D0542579

The Long Johns

The Long Johns

John Bird
and
John Fortune

HUTCHINSON
LONDON

1 3 5 7 9 10 8 6 4 2

This edition first published in 1996 by Hutchinson

Random House (UK) Limited
20 Vauxhall Bridge Road, London SW1V 2SA

Random House Australia (Pty) Limited
20 Alfred Street, Milsons Point, Sydney
New South Wales 2061, Australia

Random House New Zealand Limited
18 Poland Road, Glenfield, Auckland 10,
New Zealand

Random House South Africa (pty) Limited
Box 2263, Rosebank 2121, South Africa

A CIP record for this book is available from the British Library

Papers used by Random House UK Limited are natural, recyclable products made from wood grown in sustainable forests. The manufacturing processes conform to the environmental regulations of the country of origin.

ISBN 0 091802164

Typeset by Deltatype Ltd, Birkenhead, Merseyside
Printed and bound in Great Britain by Mackays of Chatham Plc

CONTENTS

INTRODUCTION

We do not have a script as such, so the text of these pieces comes from verbatim transcripts of the actual studio recordings. Some minor cleaning-up has been done, but only to cut out pointless repetitions of words and phrases (mostly 'I mean') which would just be irritating to read. Otherwise, what follows is what we said. Our routine on the studio day was to talk over the notes we had made during the week and have a couple of attempts at the conversation in a dressing room, one of which was usually recorded on sound tape for Geoff Atkinson to listen to. Apart from a technical check of sound and lighting we never rehearsed on the studio floor: the first time the director or any of the crew saw a piece was when we actually did it on air in front of the audience. Each conversation was done once and once only; we never re-did a piece or even a section of a piece. We only ever stopped once: in the piece about Prisons (p 47) we were, shamefully, laughing so much we had to pause for a minute to recover.

The running time of the conversations varied from about ten minutes to fifteen; for Rory Bremner's show they would be edited down to around five minutes; those shown on *The Long Johns* were left at their full length, as are all the pieces printed here. For those interested in such things, a typical camera script is shown overleaf.

ITEM 4

JOHN BIRD AND JOHN FORTUNE

(AS DIRECTED) AD LIB

It is a tribute to the wit and skill of the directors, vision mixer, camera crew, and everyone else that they caught all this, flying blind.

There are too many people we need to thank for them all to be mentioned by name. The many journalists, academics, union officials, policy institutes, and sometimes politicians themselves, who freely gave of their time and specialist knowledge. Every single person at Vera, the production company for *Rory Bremner – Who Else?* and *The Long Johns*, in particular our researchers: Rachael Barraclough on the first three series, Paul Stephenson on the fourth, together with Elissa Phipps. And we have a special debt of gratitude to the producers at Vera, Elaine Morris and Geoff Atkinson. Elaine has been particularly helpful in the preparation of this book, and it was Geoff who, while we were still working at the BBC, first suggested that we try this kind of ad-libbed conversation piece and who kept us going through our floundering attempts at it with advice and an inexhaustible flow of encouragement. Finally, whatever expression of thanks we make to Rory Bremner himself can only be inadequate. It was Rory who asked us to work with him what now seems many years ago, and we have ever since had the benefit of his support, the example of his integrity, and the inspiration of his incomparable talents.

DIARY NOTES

Fortune made some diary notes for the sixth week of Rory's series.

Monday 6th May

It takes me about an hour to drive to John's office. It's a spring day at last and trees are in flower in the suburban gardens of Ewell and Epsom. I park behind the pub and, walking back down the track, hear my first cuckoo this year. John's office is a converted kennels in the out-buildings of an old farmhouse. It consists of an outer room with lots of books and a fridge containing a choice of still and sparkling mineral water, and an inner room just big enough for a desk and two chairs. We sit in the inner room and talk about the weekend, the puppies, the weather, until one of us says, as one of us says each week, 'Well, I don't know what we're going to do this week.'

Last week's show was recorded on Thursday night. We'd done something about Labour's tax plans and John wants to do something non-political this week. He suggests the Millennium celebrations. The sum of our knowledge about the subject is British Airways' plan to build a giant ferris wheel on the South Bank, and Richard Branson's idea of tethering a balloon at Greenwich, both projects at the leading edge of innovation in air travel. We call Paul, our researcher at Vera, and ask him to dig up some cuttings on the

Millennium. After which it's time to go up to the pub for lunch before the ramblers get there.

Tuesday 7th May

Paul has faxed us lots of material. It seems that besides the big wheel and the balloon, another project has been proposed. A consortium of companies wants to build a tower 650 feet high at a cost of £91 million. It's to be called the Globorama. Visitors will travel to the top of the tower where they can watch live satellite television pictures of Sydney Harbour. This seems promising.

It's my turn to be George Parr this week and the first thing to decide is who he is. We appoint him in overall control of Millennium events and start to make some notes. We see that Virginia Bottomley, the Heritage Secretary wants the Millennium celebrations to 'embrace the whole nation in a shared vision'. We wonder what could unite the nation in such warm friendly feelings and arrive eventually at the Queen Mother. And if not the dear lady herself then a 300-foot inflatable Queen Mother towed over London behind a Spitfire.

I ask John what he expects to be doing on the last night of the century and he says going to bed and pulling the blankets over his head. This seems like another way of uniting the country, an appropriate ceremony to involve everyone. It seems a possible way of ending the piece. Off to the pub for lunch.

Wednesday 8th May

I find John hunched over a fax Paul sent last night. It's a story from the *Independent on Sunday* last March. The Millennium Commission has chosen a site at Greenwich on which to build a Great Exhibition. British Gas owns the land, which is derelict and heavily polluted by cyanides, sulphur compounds and phenols. A Government Agency called English Partnerships is thought to be paying £20 million towards decontaminating the site.[1] The Chairman of English Partnerships, Lord Walker, also happens to be a director of British Gas. Planning permission has been granted to build 3000 houses, a business park and shops when the Exhibition is over, so that the currently worthless land will later be worth between £250,000 and £500,000 an acre.

Here are two ironies. The tiny one that we wanted to do a light, frothy piece about something completely non-political but here we are again up to our knees in muddy waters. And the larger one that a national celebration of a new century should involve a property deal, an ex-cabinet minister and a privatised utility company. *Plus ça change. . . .*

Tomorrow we'll go to the studios in Wembley, try doing the conversation a couple of times, record one on tape for Geoff and around 8.15 in the evening do it for the audience. On Monday I'll drive down to John's and say, at some point, 'Well, I don't know what we're going to do this week.'

[1] For an update, see p. 242

ARMS PROCUREMENT

The seeds for this piece were planted in a conversation we had on 14 November 1994 with Anthony Sampson. He mentioned the little-known fact that in 1988 an extra £1 billion of public money was made available to the Export Credit Guarantee department specifically to boost large overseas defence sales. ECGs ensure that if the exporting company doesn't get paid, the British taxpayer foots the bill. 1988 marked the end of the Iran-Iraq War. The possibility that we might have paid for weapons subsequently used against us suggested avenues worth exploring, and during that week we spoke to a number of people connected with 'defence', as it is amusingly called. One of them was an extremely senior civil servant, who remarked, 'It's just part of the fog of hypocrisy which surrounds this place.' Oh, right. So long as we know.

Bird Sir George Parr, you are a distinguished businessman, who has been seconded recently to the Ministry of Defence from a well-known firm of arms manufacturers.

Fortune Now let me stop you right there.

Bird Sorry?

Fortune Are you trying to insinuate something?

Bird No, no no. I, I was just . . .

Fortune I mean are you implying that I'm some sort of sleazy merchant of death?

Bird No, no, I was just saying that you are a distinguished businessman who has just been seconded to the Ministry of Defence from a well-known firm of arms manufacturers.

Fortune So you mean it in a complimentary way?

Bird Yes, yes, absolutely.

Fortune Well carry on then.

Bird Right, well, well some people would say that um, you sleazy merchants of death are continuing to supply more arms to . . . why do we need all these arms? Why do we need all these new weapons systems?

Fortune Well that's very simple, we need them to defend our country.

Bird Yes.

Fortune And of course we need an arms industry to replace those bits of equipment, aircraft, Tornado bombers, that sort of thing, that are lost, unfortunately, in action.

Bird Well yes, you say that, I mean I know we lost six Tornadoes in the Gulf War, but we haven't lost any in Bosnia, so . . .

Fortune No, I'm talking about the United Kingdom. We've lost seven Tornadoes in the last three months.

Bird Is there a war going on in the United Kingdom, which I don't know about?

Fortune Not so far as I'm aware, no. And I think we in the Ministry of Defence would be among the first to know if there were a war going on.

Bird If there were a war going on . . . Why have these seven . . .

Fortune No these seven aircraft have been lost unfortunately in training exercises.

Bird What, in the last year?

Fortune So far this year, yes.

Bird That's rather a lot, isn't it?

Fortune Well these losses are inevitable, although the aeroplanes, as you probably know, cost twenty million pounds each, but we haven't . . .

Bird That's a hundred and forty million pounds of aircraft which have sort of crashed . . .

Fortune Yes, I'm not very good at figures, but it must be something like that.

Bird They've been lost in training have they?

Fortune Yes, because you see we have to train our pilots to fly very very low.

Bird Why?

Fortune So that they're under an enemy radar.

Bird Yes.

Fortune If they were above the radar then there is a real possibility that one or two of these machines could be lost.

Bird So I see, so we're training these pilots to fly under the radar of a non-existent enemy in order to avoid them being lost, and then they're lost, are they, in training?

Fortune Absolutely lost, yes . . . You see the logic?

Bird I do see, yes, I do see the logic of that.

Fortune And of course it's not only Tornadoes that have to be replaced.

Bird No no. There are weapons systems of all kinds.

Fortune Absolutely, I mean guided missile systems, they are often needing to be replaced because we fire them off.

Bird Yes, but of course they don't actually *crash* do they, I mean . . .

Fortune No, no, but they very rarely come back. And in fact if they did come back it would be a disaster.

Bird Yes. And they'd be a write-off, those weapons, anyway.

Fortune Yes.

Bird Well, but can we just say . . . at the Ministry of Defence, I mean you having specialized knowledge as a former arms manufacturer, what happens? If say the RAF decides they want a new surface to air missile system, for example, what . . .

Fortune Well in that case I would say to them: 'I think what you need is is something like the British Aerospace Rapier 2000.'

Bird I see.

Fortune And then they would say: 'Do we know anyone who makes something like that . . ?'

Bird And what would you say?

Fortune I'd say: 'Well, I can't say off the top of my head, but . . . I know it's a long shot, why don't I call British Aerospace . . .'

Bird Yes.

Fortune . . . And ask them if they make anything like that.

Bird And then what?

Fortune And they tell me that by a tremendous stroke of luck they make something called the British Aerospace Rapier 2000.

Bird I see, yes. Well that is a coincidence isn't it? So then of course you have to negotiate a price.

Fortune Yes, because our greatest priority of course is value for money for the British taxpayer. We mustn't pay a penny more than we have to.

Bird Hmmm, yes, so . . .

Fortune So then I suggest I ring up British Aerospace and say: 'How much are you asking for these weapons?'

Bird Yes . . .

Fortune And then I realise that I don't have to ask them how much they want for the weapons, because I already know.

Bird Do you?

Fortune Yes.

Bird How do you know that?

Fortune Because up until last Friday I was Chairman of British Aerospace.

Bird I see, and after that you were seconded to the Ministry of Defence?

Fortune That's right.

Bird So does your work stop there?

Fortune No no, that's the easy part . . . That's the part I can do in my sleep.

Bird Is it?

Fortune And indeed, frequently do. So now comes the hard negotiation to get the best possible deal for the British taxpayer.

Bird Of course.

Fortune Do you know about unit costs?

Bird Yes. [PAUSE] No, I don't know about unit costs.

Fortune Well I'll explain it to you. Supposing the RAF needs twenty of these weapon systems and they cost say ten million pounds each. Now if I could persuade British Aerospace to make two hundred of these systems, then the cost to the RAF would go down to eight million pounds each, and that would represent a tremendous saving for the British taxpayer.

Bird No it wouldn't, because instead of spending two hundred million pounds on the twenty we need, we'd be spending one point six billion pounds on two hundred of them, a hundred and eighty of which we didn't need.

[PAUSE]

Fortune Yes.

Bird Yes.

Fortune Yes, but you see what we have to do then is to export the surplus one hundred and eighty . . .

Bird Oh, I see . . .

Fortune And that is how we get the unit cost saving to the British taxpayer. Let me give you a concrete example of this. During the Gulf War, we were able to deploy highly sophisticated weapons against Iraq precisely because we had exported the very same weapons to other countries.

Bird Which other countries in particular?

Fortune Well at that time, principally Iraq.

Bird Yes, I see. So, Iraq was using against us weapons which we had sold to it?

Fortune Yes, and this represents a tremendous triumph for the sales teams . . .

Bird Yes, I see . . .

Fortune . . . both of the companies involved and the British Government, because the weapons that we've sold in such large numbers, all round the world, were often to countries who simply couldn't afford to pay for them.

Bird Yes, it *is* a triumph to sell to countries who can't afford to pay for them. [PAUSE] How is that done?

Fortune Well it involves a solution which is called the Export Credit Guarantee.

Bird Hmmm.

Fortune Which works like this: if a company sells something to a foreign government, and that foreign government fails to pay for it, then the company is reimbursed from the Export Credit Guarantee fund.

Bird I see, yes.

Fortune Which is paid by the Government.

Bird And that applies to arms as well does it?

Fortune Oh yes, even in the last year over half of the Export Credit Guarantees covered armaments.

Bird And how much does that involve?

Fortune Just about two billion pounds.

Bird Yes. And which sort of countries do we use that system for?

Fortune Well Iraq for one.

Bird Iraq?

Fortune Yes.

Bird Right, so, let me just see if I've got this absolutely straight: we sell arms to Iraq, which Iraq have used against us, and we have paid for them?

Fortune You've got it.

Bird Right.

Fortune Yes, because if they hadn't known that we were going to pay for them, they wouldn't have bought them in the first place, would they?

Bird I suppose not. Well Saddam Hussein must have been a tricky customer to deal with, mustn't he, rather difficult?

Fortune Surprisingly not.

Bird Oh really?

Fortune No, he agreed to any price that we asked, basically.

Bird Oh. Well I suppose if he knew that that you were going to pay for them, then he would agree to any price. Have you taken any steps to recover the money for them?

Fortune Oh certainly, we take steps all the time.

Bird Really?

Fortune Even this week I wrote to him in the strongest terms.

Bird Did you?

Fortune I've got the letter, do you want me to . . . ?

Bird Yes, yes, certainly.

Fortune Do you want to see it?

Bird So this is top secret?

Fortune Well, it's open government I believe in.

Bird Yes.

[HE IS HANDED THE LETTER,

AND READS]

'Dear Mr Hussein, we have been looking for our files and can find no record of a payment from you of the £652 million still outstanding for exports from the United Kingdom. As a valued customer, you will no doubt wish to correct this oversight in the near future. I can appreciate that you have had pressing matters that have engaged your attention, but as soon as you have finished gassing your fellow countrymen, perhaps you could favour us with an early response.
If you have settled this account within the last few days, please ignore this letter.
We take this opportunity of enclosing our Autumn Catalogue, and draw your attention to our improved napalm range on page 8.'
Well yes, that's a very severe, very very tough stuff . . .

Fortune Yes.

Bird Yes. So, this is obviously very good for a flourishing British arms industry.

Fortune Absolutely.

Bird But don't you think that after an election this might all come to an end . . . ?

Fortune Oh no. No no, the Labour Party's as keen on the armaments industry as the Conservatives, because after all, 120,000 jobs are involved, and the unions within the industry are very very keen on it.

Bird Yes, well, thank you very much Sir George.

XENOPHOBIA

We can modestly claim to have set a trend here. We had been thinking for over a year about doing a piece based on the equation 'Euro-scepticism = Xenophobia' and we recorded this on 16 May, 1996. The following week John Major announced his policy of non-cooperation with the European Union over the BSE issue and was cheered to the echo by his own backbenchers, and supported by Labour. The *Daily Express* took its whole front page to proclaim 'Major speaks for Britain' and the *Sun* published twenty handy hints for insulting German tourists.

Fortune Sir George Parr, you're a Conservative back-bench MP, on the Euro-sceptic wing of your party.

Bird Well, I don't like that word, 'Euro-sceptic', really. I think it's long past its sell-by date.

Fortune You don't like the 'sceptic' part, it's sort of negative do you feel?

Bird It's a bit negative, really, for what we really represent now. I think we should be talking about much more positive, more fundamental things.

Fortune I see, so . . .

Bird Fundamental principles.

Fortune I see, so these principles, how would they be carried through into policy, I mean are you in favour of complete withdrawal from the Union, or do you want a free-trade area, or . . . ?

Bird Well, you see once again, these are side issues, we get bogged down in these, these technicalities of convergence criteria, and subsidiarity and so forth. I think we should say what we mean.

Fortune I see, well that's refreshing. And what in fact do you mean?

Bird Well, as I say, I was talking about positive fundamental principles, by which I mean something very deep in the British character.

Fortune Yes . . . ?

Bird Which we are in danger of losing, which is under threat, and which I think could be summed up as a proud, traditional and instinctive loathing of foreigners.

Fortune Well that's . . . that's very honest of you, really, to say so.

Bird Well, we are an honest people, the British are an honest people. I don't take any personal credit for that.

Fortune No. No, that's just part of our character.

Bird Just part of being British, yes.

Fortune I see, yes. Might it be objected that that point of view is in itself, ah, xenophobic?

Bird Well, again, I don't like the word 'xenophobic', it suggests irrational prejudice. And of course it's a Greek word, and I detest Greeks. We are talking here about plain historical fact, for example, that Germans are Nazis, and we beat them in the war, at a time when the French cravenly surrendered, the Italians behaved with their usual despicable cowardice, the Belgians allowed themselves to be overrun by anybody who happened to be passing. The Portuguese were all spies, and the Spanish of course kept out of it, they spent the whole war throwing donkeys off the top of church towers.

Fortune Yes. You haven't . . . you haven't mentioned Luxembourg in that.

Bird Well, well I don't know much about the people of Luxembourg, though I imagine their women's armpits aren't anything to write home about, but I . . .

Fortune Aren't you in fact there saying in a round-about way that these foreigners are inferior?

Bird Oh no, no no, no, I think that would be . . . no, that would be misconstruing what I have said. I think the British are superior, which is a different thing.

Fortune Superior in what sense?

Bird Well, tolerance. For example, we're very tolerant people, we take people as we find them, on the whole.

Fortune Yes. Forgive me, but you don't seem very tolerant to me . . .

Bird Well I don't see why, I mean if these foreigners *want* to be devious and arrogant, and corrupt, by all means let them.

Fortune Yes.

Bird So long as they don't tell us what to do, you see, and they don't interfere in the running of our affairs.

Fortune What aspect of their interference do you dislike most?

Bird Well virtually every aspect. Let's take an example. The courts, the European Court of Human Rights, for example, as we know is a puppet of the European Union, and it told us about, you know, not shooting IRA suspects in Gibraltar. Now frankly, I don't think any court of the European Union should tell me who I can and cannot shoot on Crown territory, it's as simple as that.

Fortune Yes, but in fact the European Court of Human Rights has got nothing to do with the European Union, has it?

Bird That doesn't alter my argument.

Fortune Why not?

Bird Nothing alters my arguments really.

Fortune Yes, I'm beginning to . . . get that view. Perhaps you were confusing the Court of Human Rights with the European Court of Justice, which *is* part of the European Union.

Bird Oh, is it? Yes, well there again you see, the European Court of Justice, has just recently forced me to fire my butler.

Fortune I can't remember a judgement that, er . . .

Bird Well not specifically on that, no, but it came within their judgement about the forty-eight-hour maximum working week. Now you can't employ a butler for a maximum of 48 hours a week, it's a nonsense. So Jenkins had to go, and now he's, I don't know, living in a cardboard box somewhere, I . . .

Fortune It must be a great change for him.

Bird No, he had a very nice cardboard box in my house next to the dog in the kitchen. But now he hasn't got a job, and the thing is that my dinner guests are now waited on by a fourteen-year-old Peruvian girl, who's got a very limited command of English and dirty fingernails.

Fortune But she's prepared to work longer hours.

Bird She works a 155-hour week, but that is because she's an illegal immigrant.

And I think it's appalling that I have been put in the position of having to break the law in order to fulfil a European directive of this kind.

Fortune And of course it is the European Court of Justice which is underpinning the whole legality of the ban on British exports of beef, isn't it?

Bird Oh well I mean I . . . I don't know what to say about that, I mean that's totally . . . I don't know what we have an army for, really. We have told these people, plainly and simply, that all British beef is completely safe, and not just that, but that some British beef is even more completely safe than . . . than other completely safe British beef.

Fortune Yes, but they feel that we haven't taken enough steps to eradicate BSE.

Bird But what do they know about BSE, frankly, on the continent? There've been 17 cases of BSE in France, we've had 160,000.

Fortune So we must know more about it.

Bird Of course, of course we do.

Fortune But in fact, in France, when they do isolate a case of BSE they slaughter the whole herd.

Bird Well of course they hate animals on the continent. I mean, look at the way the Spanish treat their cattle, they wave capes at them, and stick these, these things in them with with tassels on the end. At least we give our cattle a sporting chance of killing people.

Fortune In the long run.

Bird In the long run, yes.

Fortune So what do you think we should be doing?

Bird Well we should be standing up to them, in a way which has not been done so far. Now I'm as strong and loyal a supporter of John Major as anybody, but he is the most craven apology for a person that you can possibly imagine. I mean he . . . when Herr Nazi Kohl came over, he gave this lunch and served beef, but, he said, you can have chicken if you want. That's no good. The only person standing up to these people, is, and thank God for it, Her Majesty the Queen who, when the garlic-eating person arrived, said . . . .

Fortune Chirac.

Bird Chirac, he had to eat beef.

Fortune Yes. He didn't have any alternative. He just had to . . .

Bird He didn't have any alternative.

Fortune And you approve of that sort of symbolic gesture?

Bird I think it's more than symbolic, I think that the Queen and God bless her for it, was prepared to risk her, herself and her whole household dying a hideous and lingering death in order to make her point, to . . .

Fortune So obviously what's most important to you is the idea of sovereignty, isn't it?

Bird Well no, what's most important to me is hating foreigners, but after that, yes, the idea of sovereignty.

Fortune And you feel that our destiny should be in our hands . . .

Bird Of course.

Fortune The laws, the management of our economy, and I suppose defence, would be . . .

Bird Defence, defence in particular, yes.

Fortune So you'd be very much against any further integration of our forces with those of Europe?

Bird Without any question. The control over the defence of our kingdom should remain where it is at the moment: in the hands of the United States of America.

Fortune Sir George Parr, thank you very much indeed.

ROYALS

It used to be said, and not so long ago, that you shouldn't attack the Royal Family because 'they can't answer back'. If only that were true: now they do little else. However, this was not an attack, so much as an attempt to try and find a way forward. For her, for him, for them, for all of us.

The occasion was the publication of an 'authorised' biography of Prince Charles by David Dimbleby, or was it Jonathan? Which itself followed the publication of a 'sort of authorised' biography of Princess Diana by Andrew Morton, or was it Jelly Roll?

Anyway, seconds out.

Fortune Sir George Parr, you are, and have been for many years, a very senior member of the Royal household, advising the Queen at Buckingham Palace.

Bird Yes, I have had that privilege.

Fortune Now, can I just put this point to you, the Monarchy is in a terrible mess isn't it?

Bird Well, I must choose my words very carefully here. Yes.

Fortune And who do you think essentially is responsible for this?

Bird I think as far as the present situation goes . . . I feel I must say that the parents I think are to blame, and in particular the father. You know when you have sons, and it's sort of drummed into them from a very early age that they're somehow special and above the common herd, well, eventually they get to believe it, you know, they think they can do anything they want. So I do think Richard Dimbleby has a lot to answer for.

Fortune I thought for one moment there you were going to say Prince Philip.

Bird Oh good heavens, perish the thought, no no.

Fortune No?

Bird No no, Prince Philip is of course a very . . . has a very special place in the Crown, and I think what you have to remember about Prince Philip, and I've known him for many years, is that he is a very, *very* unpleasant man. A total shit, in fact. And that's always made it very difficult for us in the Palace of course.

Fortune Yes. It has been suggested in the Dimbleby book that he was something of a bully towards his son, especially concerning his marriage.

Bird Well of course this was a very difficult time for us all, I must give him that . . . we're talking about a time when the Prince was barely into adolescence, and he was . . .

Fortune He was thirty-two, wasn't he?

Bird Yes, and as I say, barely into adolescence. And he, you know, hardly knew how to walk straight, but we had to find a wife for him, and not just a wife of course . . .

Fortune No. Someone who was going to be a future Queen of England.

Bird Exactly. We were looking for someone very special, a future Queen, and of course there has to be very strict criteria about that.

Fortune Naturally.

Bird She has to be upper-class, of course, because the Royal Family isn't very upper-class so it's very good to have . . .

Fortune That element of . . .

Bird . . . that element in it . . .

Fortune . . . of good breeding.

Bird . . . she has to be very presentable, and of course a virgin. Now . . .

Fortune She has to be a virgin?

Bird Of course, yes. And . . .

Fortune This presumably was because in this particular case the, the Prince himself was sexually inexperienced?

Bird No, what is necessary is for the *bride* to be sexually inexperienced, but the bridegroom has to be sexually experienced.

Fortune And why is that?

Bird It's more fun I suppose. I mean for a man it's more fun.

Fortune For the man?

Bird Yes.

Fortune So, so you set about . . . as a team of advisers . . .

Bird Yes.

Fortune . . . looking for . . .

Bird Trying to, it was difficult you see to find . . . I mean virgins are rather thin on the ground in the circles that I move in, and we had basically a two-pronged assault on this question. We had what you might call a hands-on approach, and that involved sending Major James Hewitt, or Corporal Hewitt as he was at that time, out into debs' balls and point-to-points and so on looking for virgins.

Fortune Yes.

Bird But that wasn't totally successful. Partly because every time he found a virgin, in some curious way five minutes later she wasn't a virgin any more. I don't quite know how, we never understood that.

Fortune It was a sort of self-cancelling operation.

Bird Exactly. And so then the other approach we took was to put a discreet advertisement in *The Times.*

Fortune In *The Times?*

Bird Yes.

Fortune What did that say?

Bird Well of course it had to be very discreetly worded indeed. It said, 'If anybody has had sexual intercourse with Lady Diana Spencer of Althorpe, please ring this number in strict confidence.'

Fortune And did anyone ring?

Bird Well no, no, no. We waited and waited, it was rather like the IRA ceasefire actually.

Fortune To see if eventually the virginity issue became permanent.

Bird The clock ticked, and the virginity eventually was regarded as permanent.

Fortune As permanent.

Bird Yes. While at that time there were people actually who put themselves forward.

Fortune What, as future queens?

Bird As future queens, Arianna Stassinopoulous was one.

Fortune Really?

Bird We considered that, but we all thought well, it's not a frightfully good idea, we've already got one pushy, social climbing, sex-mad Greek in the family, um, and . . .

Fortune So you . . .

Bird So we didn't pursue that avenue.

Fortune But despite all of your efforts, you, a highly trained team of advisers . . .

Bird Oh yes, yes. The Queen, has always had a very distinguished, very experienced team of advisers, to advise her . . .

Fortune The Queen has?

Bird Absolutely.

Fortune But you got it completely wrong.

Bird Totally wrong, absolutely.

Fortune Yes.

Bird Well you win a few, you lose a few.

Fortune Yes, I suppose that's true. And now we have the very distressing spectacle of two embattled camps.

Bird Yes.

Fortune We have the Prince's camp and the Princess's camp throwing mud and accusations at each other, that must be a tragic spectacle.

Bird Well, yes, of course, I would sooner not deal in the personalities involved. I work at Buckingham Palace and I prefer not to think about the personalities. And in any case, I wouldn't like to choose between a flapping-eared, cello-sawing egomaniac on the one hand, and a vomiting, hysterical shopaholic on the other. I prefer to think of them not as being personalities, but as being an institution.

Fortune An institution. Yes.

Bird And it could be argued that they would be better *in* an institution, but . . .

Fortune But even so, the institution of Monarchy, you must admit, is affected in some way by the personalities of those people involved in it.

Bird Oh yes.

Fortune I mean people have behaved very appallingly.

Bird Well I have to agree with you, it's been very destructive, very very poor, very very bad behaviour. We have to put it in perspective of course, I mean we're not talking about Government ministers here, but still, it has been very bad I think. But, the trouble is of course that people outside . . . outsiders have been cashing in on this.

Fortune Yes, you're speaking of people like Andrew Morton . . .

Bird Yes.

Fortune And Pasternak. And all those sorts of people . . .

Bird All those sorts of people, the media are making an absolute fortune out of this appalling behaviour, and I think that's wrong.

Fortune It is wrong.

Bird And we've got to put a stop to that, because after all, the Royal Family do have, or should have, rights.

Fortune Well they have a right of privacy, presumably?

Bird	Yes, but I was thinking more of publishing rights. You see I think that they should have the rights to publish these things themselves. After all, it is their behaviour which is causing all this interest, I mean people all over the world are intensely interested . . .
Fortune	Well they are, yes.
Bird	. . . in our Royal Family.
Fortune	Yes.
Bird	And they come over and they spend lots and lots of money, I mean they're not interested in the Dutch Royal Family are they?
Fortune	Why is that do you think?
Bird	Well because the Dutch Royal Family are decent, straightforward, and hard-working, and . . .
Fortune	They ride bicycles.
Bird	We have a tremendous asset, if we look at it in a certain way, in the behaviour of our Royal Family, we've got, we've got all sorts of things. We've got adulterers, fornicators, plagiarists, foot-fetishists, gays . . .

Fortune Lunatics.

Bird Alcoholics, lunatics, plagiarists.

Fortune Plagiarists.

Bird No, I've already said plagiarists.

Fortune No I thought I said plagiarists.

Bird No no, I think I said plagiarists actually.

Fortune Well, never mind.

Bird There's something in the Royal Family for everyone, to suit every taste you see, and I think that if . . .

Fortune But what would you say . . .

Bird . . . if we were to exploit this . . .

Fortune In a commercial sense?

Bird Yes.

Fortune You feel that this is the way that the Monarchy is going to evolve in the future?

Bird I think the Monarchy should reflect the ethos and the values of the Britain of the day.

Fortune And what is the predominant value that the Monarchy reflects in this country at the moment?

Bird Well, to make as much money as you can in the shortest possible time.

Fortune Yes, but besides that, hasn't the Monarchy also got to embody a sense of continuity?

Bird Of course.

Fortune In the nation.

Bird Yes, that's always been the case, and I think that continuity, we do have that still, and it's embodied now in the little Princes William and Harry.

Fortune Yes.

Bird They're going to give us the continuity: they're going to have a really appalling childhood, they're already having one. Followed probably by a disastrous adolescence.

Fortune Very probably, yes.

Bird And guilt, and angst, and anxiety . . .

Fortune Yes.

Bird . . . which almost certainly will involve a lot of, eventually, broken lives and broken marriages, and the rest of it, and so it will provide interest for the media as far into the future as we can possibly see.

Fortune Sir George Parr, thank you very much.

Bird It's a pleasure, thank you.

PRISONS

We did this piece in October 1995, the week that Michael Howard fired Derek Lewis from his post as Director-General of the Prison Service; this in turn followed the publication of the Learmont Report into the Parkhurst Prison escapes which had taken place in January that year. The Learmont Report is well worth a look, not least for its tasteful cover, with a pen-and-ink wash showing a Prison Officer walking round a perimeter fence with his dog. Unusually, nobody was climbing over the fence at the time the artist was at work.

Although there is much to laugh at in the Report's account of conditions at Parkhurst, there is also the sense of people – Governors and Officers – trying to do an impossible job in appalling conditions, with abysmal leadership from Headquarters and the Home Office. The blizzard of paperwork (which Learmont mentions) falling on Prison Governors is illustrated by a document in our research file for this piece: it is a copy of an Instruction to Governors, Issue Number IG48/1995 which 'amends and replaces IG39/1995, all copies of which should be destroyed'. It is dated 11th May, which means it was the forty-eighth such 'Instruction' received by Governors in four-and-a-half months. No wonder one Governor told the Learmont Inquiry:

> 'Headquarters, now grossly oversized, creates nothing but work, issues absurd directives to local prison

management and sees prison management as serving it rather than the other way round.'

Not to be outdone, the Learmont Report made 127 recommendations.

Fortune George Parr, you're the Governor of a maximum security prison.

Bird Yes.

Fortune And it's been a difficult week for the prison service.

Bird We've had our ups and downs, yes.

Fortune You mean the prisoners going up over the wall and down the other side?

Bird No, I was thinking in terms of the general morale in the service. Last week at the Tory Party Conference, the Home Secretary said, 'Prison works'.

Fortune Yes.

Bird And then this week he said that prisons were in such a shambles he was going to have to fire the Director General. So . . .

Fortune So you are rather depressed?

Bird A bit.

Fortune Because the Learmont report, which was published this week, does identify several managerial problems in the prison service. The fact that Governors like you are surrounded by this huge mountain of paper every week.

Bird Yes.

Fortune I believe one jail said that they received two hundred and thirty letters, forty-five faxes, and six E-Mail messages in one day alone.

Bird In one day, yes. That was a good jail, I wish I worked there.

Fortune But this is a great problem isn't it?

Bird Well it is a problem, and not only that, but General Learmont also pointed out and criticised the fact that we have currently, from prison headquarters, thirty-eight separate new initiatives, policy initiatives that we have to be carrying out at the present time.

Fortune Yes. He did also identify certain security problems at Parkhurst, where the three men escaped, didn't he?

Bird Yes, well of course I'm not Governor of Parkhurst, and so I can't really comment. I don't know what goes on in Parkhurst prison, I mean I hardly know what goes on in my prison, to be honest with you, I've got so much paperwork.

Fortune But for example, he did say that there was a D Wing, which was a no-go area for the warders.

Bird That's right, yes.

Fortune And that the staff in the emergency control room failed to notice on the television monitors the three prisoners climbing over the . . .

Bird Going over the wall, yes but . . .

Fortune . . . over the wall.

Bird This is partly you see a matter of resources, because he did also point out in the report that the people on duty, the officers on duty in the control room were not fully trained.

Fortune What would that training amount to?

Bird Well, we train people over a long period. We bring them into the control room and say: 'those are television screens, you probably aren't familiar with them, but they are television screens, and what you do is sit and point yourself at them, so that you can see them. And they'll be showing pictures of the prison fence, and if you happen to see little figures crawling up the wall, then you know . . .'

Fortune Alarm bells should start ringing in your head.

Bird Yes. Or preferably in the prison.

Fortune Then of course Mr Marriot, the Governor of Parkhurst jail, his whole regime was somewhat criticised wasn't it?

Bird Well it's very easy to criticise Mr Marriot, and Governors like him, for, I mean for things like having ice-cream vans in the prison, and having barbecues for the prisoners. It sounds like a woolly-minded liberal regime, but there are security benefits to these things.

Fortune In what way?

Bird Well the barbecues, for example, are a very good way for prisoner officers to meet the prisoners, to actually get to know them you see. They never get to know the ones in D Wing, because they can never get into D Wing.

Fortune Because it's a no-go area?

Bird Exactly. The prisoners won't allow them. So um . . .

Fortune So they could invite . . .

Bird You can point out . . . you can say, you see that man over there eating the flaming sausage, that is Strangler Jarvis, or whoever it might happen to be, he's a very, er, he's a very desperate and dangerous prisoner.

Fortune Yes, he would be.

Bird So it's . . .

Fortune Yes. So it is a lesson in prisoner recognition.

Bird Yes.

Fortune Being able to recognise a prisoner when you actually see him . . .

Bird Yes. It is, it is very valuable for prisoner officers to recognise prisoners.

Fortune	Well I can see that that would be an enormous advantage.
Bird	Because they might recognise them in the street. It was pointed out by General Learmont, of course, that after the Parkhurst escape one of the escapees was passed in the street by a prisoner officer who didn't recognise him. And so it is very useful if you're out in the street and you're a prison officer and you see a prisoner coming out of the newsagents, and, and you think, well hang on, hang on . . .
Fortune	I've seen him somewhere before.
Bird	Yes.
Fortune	It must have been at the barbecue.
Bird	At the barbecue. Precisely.
Fortune	That would be very useful, one could see that, especially if the man coming out of the newsagents was carrying the till. But . . .
Bird	Yes. Indeed.
Fortune	If one could get back for a moment to the Home Secretary, Michael Howard, I mean would you say, as some have, that there has been too

much interference by the Home Secretary in the administration of prisons?

Bird Well yes, I mean that has been said, but it's very good to have a hands-on Home Secretary, somebody who takes an interest. And we always looked forward to his visits to the prison, they weren't very frequent, but he always had something to say to everybody. He would say, you know, 'what are you in for?' And I'd say 'I'm the Governor.' And then he'd say 'thank you very much and goodbye.' Or occasionally; 'thank you very much and you're fired.'

Fortune I was thinking more of the gap which has been identified, this week particularly, between what's called policy and what's called operational matters.

Bird It's difficult to make the division there. I mean previously we've always thought that 'policy' was pretending to the voters you knew how to deal with crime, and 'operational' was pretending to your staff that you knew how to deal with criminals. But now, a rather more simplified definition is that policy is when things are going all right, and operational is when they aren't.

Fortune But let's just say, for the moment, that Michael Howard really meant what he said, that he was, in other words, he was telling the truth, he wasn't lying.

Bird We have to assume that do we?

Fortune Yes.

Bird For the purposes of this argument?

Fortune Yes, just . . .

Bird Yes. Wait a minute, give me a minute. [PAUSE] It's rather like watching *The X-Files* isn't it?

Fortune Take as long as you want.

Bird Yes all right, no no, I've got it, I've got it.

Fortune So so, if he actually means . . .

Bird Yes, he's telling the truth, I'm holding on to that . . .

Fortune . . . all these things about sentences and sending people down for life and two strikes and you're out, and that sort of thing, then the prison population is just going to rise exponentially, isn't it . . . ?

Bird Oh, yes. We already have one of the highest prison populations in the world, we have 51,000 people in prison[1], and of course it will go up to twice that, three times, four times.

Fortune And it's going to be ruinously expensive.

Bird It is.

Fortune We can't afford it.

Bird We can't, well . . .

Fortune Because we'd have to build new prisons and . . .

Bird We'd have to build new prisons, but even, even if you don't count building new prisons and so forth, it still costs, for example in my prison, on average, it costs £816 a week to keep a prisoner.

Fortune So that's £40,000 . . .

Bird £43,000 a year. Now, I've come up with an idea, which I've put forward

[1] True when we did the piece (October 1995). At the time of going to press, in July 1996, the number had risen to 56,000.

to the Home Office. What you do is say all right, it's forty-three thousand pounds, half of that is, well let's say twenty-two thousand pounds, so you go to a prisoner and you say: 'Look here. Would you like to make twenty-two thousand pounds? We'll pay you eleven thousand down now, you go out, you don't commit any crimes or anything for a year and then you get another eleven thousand on top of that.' And now this, at a stroke you see, will halve your prison budget.

Fortune Yes you would. And you wouldn't need the other half because you wouldn't have anyone in the prisons . . .

Bird There wouldn't be any crime.

Fortune And there wouldn't be any crime, no.

Bird It's a good idea isn't it?

Fortune That's rather . . . The only flaw in that, in that otherwise terribly ingenious piece of social engineering is that there isn't a punishment element.

Bird No, there isn't a punishment element, and of course a lot of people want that. A lot of people want that more than anything else, they want the . . .

Fortune More than not wanting any crime?

Bird More than not wanting any crime, more than wanting justice, for example.

Fortune Yes.

Bird They want punishment. So in that case we will have to do what has been suggested anyway, by Learmont and others, which is to introduce American systems.

Fortune Oh yes, this is the Super Max prison.

Bird The Super Max prison, for the most violent prisoners, all in one place.

Fortune I see.

Bird Except, well, with any luck some of the inmates will kill each other.

Fortune That would be a help.

Bird It would be a help, yes.

Fortune And of course the Boot Camps.

Bird The Boot Camps, where we put undisciplined . . .

Fortune Yobs.

Bird . . . yob teenagers, and turn them out as highly disciplined, fit, aggressive, criminals.

Fortune Yes.

Bird And chain-gangs and tagging and the rest of it.

Fortune Do you think that these American ideas would work in this country?

Bird Well, as we all know, there's very little crime in America. So I . . .

Fortune Yes, I think that's true isn't it?

Bird So I imagine they'll be as successful here as they are there.

Fortune Yes, because this is the first priority of any prison service, isn't it, is to prevent crime, to . . .

Bird No, the first priority of the prison service is that whatever happens Michael Howard isn't to blame for it.

Fortune George Parr, thank you very much indeed.

Bird It's a pleasure, thank you.

POST OFFICE

John Fortune played Bill Cockburn, then Chief Executive of the Post Office, who was engaged at the time (Autumn 1994) in a campaign to persuade the Government to privatize it. From the *Sunday Telegraph*, 28 August 1994:

> 'According to figures compiled by a former director of Royal Mail . . . £1.8 million has been spent in the last three months on external agency, material and staff time costs to drum up support for privatization. £1m of it has gone on briefings for Post Office staff, while seven regional conferences involving more than 5,000 managers added another £350,000 to the bill. A further £100,000 was paid out to consultants for their services at these events while more than £150,000 was spent on lobbying, brochures, in-house publications, and freephone and business reply services.'

From the Post Office's Policy on Ethics:

> 'Funds and resources may not be used, directly or indirectly, for partisan purposes. These include party or campaign funds, or any improper attempts to influence a political decision.'

In the event, the Post Office was not privatised.

Bird The future of the Post Office is very

much in the balance and Bill Cockburn, you are the Chief Executive of the Post Office.

Fortune Yes I am.

Bird And, again . . . can I call you Bill?

Fortune No.

Bird The problem for the Government is they were going to announce this week whether the Post Office was going to be privatized, or partly privatized . . .

Fortune That's correct.

Bird Or kept in the Public Sector.

Fortune Yes, they should have made a decision on Monday, the Cabinet Committee involved should have made it then, but it was put off until Wednesday, and then it was discussed in full Cabinet on Thursday, and we still don't have a decision, it's absolutely dreadful.

Bird It must be frustrating for you.

Fortune It's extremely frustrating. I took the step yesterday of speaking directly to the Prime Minister's office to try and get some sort of an answer.

Bird And what did he say?

Fortune Nothing really. There was a lot of sound of breaking crockery and some hysterical sobbing, but I hung up, I'm a busy man.

Bird No decision was made then. I mean how do you want it to go?

Fortune Well I want to make it absolutely clear that the ownership of the Post Office is entirely a political matter. It's a Government decision.

Bird Yes, it's not . . .

Fortune And the Post Office Board will not, and in fact cannot express an opinion because of our business code of ethics.

Bird I see. But you have spent two million pounds, haven't you, conducting a campaign in favour of privatization?

Fortune Yes, are you implying by that that by spending two million pounds campaigning for privatization we are in favour of it?

Bird Well, I mean I suppose on the face of it . . . were you saying that you could just as easily have spent two million pounds campaigning against it?

Fortune Absolutely. Or we could have spent four million pounds having two campaigns arguing for it *and* against it.

Bird Why didn't you do that?

Fortune We thought it would be a complete waste of public money.

Bird Yes, I see. So what are your reasons for . . . I mean you personally want privatization don't you?

Fortune I desperately want privatization because I don't think that anybody realises quite what an appalling situation the Post Office is in.

Bird Is it?

Fortune We're standing on the edge of a commercial abyss.

Bird But you made a £360 million profit last year.

Fortune Yes.

Bird And in fact you've made considerable profits and ever increasing profits for the last few years haven't you?

Fortune Yes.

Bird You've made profits continually for eighteen years in fact.

Fortune Absolutely true.

Bird And you are the most successful Post Office in the world, isn't that right?

Fortune We're the most profitable Post Office in the world.

Bird Yes, I see . . .

Fortune So you see don't you that we can't go on like this.

Bird Well yes, um . . .

Fortune I mean things have got to change, and change radically.

Bird Why is that, in what way?

Fortune Well we've simply got to become a private company.

Bird Yes, but a lot of people actually like the Post Office the way it is . . .

Fortune Yes.

Bird And after all it provides 180,000 jobs . . .

Fortune Yes.

Bird It provides a lot of services to people in all parts of the country . . .

Fortune Now just let me stop you there, because somehow, I don't know how, but you happen to have stumbled on exactly the point.

Bird Oh thank you.

Fortune No company in the 1990s can employ 180,000 people.

Bird No?

Fortune It's completely mad.

Bird Is it?

Fortune And what are some of them doing? Some of them are driving up to some remote farmhouse in Shetland to deliver a letter to a little old lady. And if the little old lady happens to be blind, they'd be delivering the letter without any charge at all.

Bird Really?

Fortune This is the economics of the madhouse.

Bird Is it?

Fortune Oh yes.

Bird And so what would you want to do, after privatization?

Fortune Well what I'd be forced to do is to sack about fifty thousand of the workforce, downsizing the workforce, and of course cut services.

Bird You say you would be forced to do it, why would you be forced to do it?

Fortune I'd be forced to do it because that would be my responsibility to my shareholders.

Bird Oh I see, yes. You wouldn't want to do it yourself?

Fortune Oh no, certainly not.

Bird But at the moment of course you're a public sector company, you don't have any shareholders.

Fortune Exactly.

Bird So, wait a minute, let me just see if I can get this right . . . you want to be privatized in order that you will have shareholders who will force you to sack all these people and cut all these services.

Fortune You've got there in the end.

Bird Thank you, thank you. I see, so that's the real reason is it, that . . .

Fortune No that isn't the real reason.

Bird Oh . . .

Fortune No, no no. What we must be is competitive, because I don't know if you know it, but we're getting a lot of international competition in the postal service.

Bird Oh really, other Post Offices want to take over your business?

Fortune Yes, the Dutch and the Germans want to come over here and take away our business.

Bird Yes, I can't quite see how that would work, um . . . . You're saying that a postman in Frankfurt, say, would wake up in the morning, and say 'I've got to go off on my postal round in Surbiton'?

Fortune These foreigners will do anything. And it's, it's not only the international competition.

Bird It's not just the international competition?

Fortune Oh no. No no. No no.

Bird Well wait a minute, er, sorry, what else is there?

Fortune Well I don't want to be a scaremonger at all, but, and this is rather sensitive commercial intelligence . . .

Bird Yes.

Fortune . . . But it may have crossed your mind, even yours, that we may not be alone in the universe.

Bird I see, so you're suggesting that a part of your Post Office business might be taken over by . . . by alien life forms?

Fortune The possibility of extra-terrestrial post offices does exist.

Bird Oh really?

Fortune Yes.

Bird And, and . . .

Fortune And they might, and I'm sure, we don't know for sure, but they might have just spotted this niche in the market. And then you see we'd be in a very difficult . . .

Bird How would that work exactly?

Fortune Well I think it might involve a certain loss of customer service.

Bird In what way?

Fortune Well the aliens would have to take our mail . . .

Bird Yes.

Fortune And go somewhere across the galaxy. And . . . and sort it there, and it might take a very long time for it to get back.

Bird Yes.

Fortune Even at warp factor ten.

Bird Yes, hmmm. So you you want to be in a position to compete with, um, alien life forms then?

Fortune Yes, and in order to do so we must have a level playing field.

Bird Yes, of course.

Fortune We must be seen to be lean and mean and green. Well perhaps not green, because they'll be green.

Bird So that's the real reason then is it for . . . ?

Fortune No that isn't the real reason.

Bird That isn't the real reason?

Fortune No no, the real reason goes back to a time in the early 80s before the telecommunications part of the Post Office was hived off.

Bird When it was still the GPO.

Fortune And at that time I had a colleague called Ian Vallance, now Sir Ian . . .

Bird Yes, he's now the Chairman of BT isn't he?

Fortune Yes, exactly, when they were privatized he became the Chairman, and I think that my deepest feelings about this can be embodied in the very real difference there is between

Sir Ian and myself.

Bird Well you mean that he has now, because it's been privatized, freedom to operate in the commercial market, and you haven't?

Fortune No. No, the real difference is that his basic salary is £663,000 a year. And mine is only £150,000.

Bird And your salary is set by the Government, of course.

Fortune Yes. Have you ever tried to live on a £150,000 a year?

Bird No.

Fortune It's next door to impossible.

Bird So, that is the real reason is it, the difference in the salaries between . . . ?

Fortune No, I think, no not entirely, because that would be rather petty, and personal. No, no, we've got to look to the future. Because you see if the Government doesn't decide to privatize now, they won't for the length of this parliament..

Bird No . . .

Fortune	And then there will be an election, and Labour will get in so it won't happen for another five years . . .
Bird	And of course they won't privatize it.
Fortune	And even if the Tories get back in after that it would be a year or so before they get round to doing anything about it, and by that time it will be 2002.
Bird	2002, yes, something like that.
Fortune	And I'll be fifty nine.
Bird	And you think that you'll be too old for the job?
Fortune	No no not that, no no, it's just that I'll only be able to pay myself a huge salary for one year before I retire, and my retirement deal will be based on that year's salary.
Bird	I see . . . yes well, that's very strategic thinking. So in fact the real reason that you want the Post Office privatized is, if I can put it, summarising it, it's a mixture of ruthlessness and greed is it?
Fortune	Well that's very nice of you to say so. Thank you very much.

Bird Not at all.

Fortune Aren't you leaving out stupidity?

Bird Sorry yes, ruthlessness, greed and stupidity. Well, thank you Bill Cockburn.

Fortune Thank you very much.

JUDGES

This is the earliest of our conversations to be included in this book: it was recorded on 4 March 1991, on the occasion of the release of the 'Birmingham Six' after serving 15 years wrongful imprisonment for an alleged IRA bombing. We are extremely grateful to the BBC, for whom the recording was made and who produced the Rory Bremner series in which it appeared, for allowing us to include this transcript.

Bird Lord Justice Merry, thank you very much for being with us this evening. Now this week three people were released from jail, three Irish people, released from jail after serving fifteen years of a twenty-five year sentence, and it was found that they hadn't committed the crime for which they'd originally been sentenced. Now in 1988 you heard their appeal, didn't you, as a member of the Court of Appeal?

Fortune I did, yes.

Bird And you turned it down.

Fortune I dismissed it.

Bird And now you find that they were in fact innocent. How do you feel about this? Personally?

Fortune Well of course it's rather awkward.

Bird Yes.

Fortune I prided myself during my years on the Bench, and before as a barrister, on being able to sum up people's characters immediately . . .

Bird Yes.

Fortune And with complete accuracy, and I must say that when I saw these three men in the dock, then I knew immediately that they were certainly guilty.

Bird Yes. You did describe them as, I think we've got it down here as 'unsavoury bog-trotters of the worst kind'. Funny, you said actually 'three men', but in fact one of them was a woman.

Fortune I'm sorry?

Bird One of them was a woman. You don't . . .

Fortune Which one?

Bird I don't know which one, I wasn't there, I mean you were there, didn't you . . .

Fortune That's absolutely extraordinary. I mean I'm perfectly sure that the police told me they were all men.

Bird Yes, but actually, I suppose they were rather a long way away from where you were sitting on the Bench . . .

Fortune Well that's true, yes. Still. Extraordinary.

Bird Yes.

Fortune She *was* Irish, wasn't she?

Bird Oh yes, she was Irish, yes.

Fortune So they got that bit right.

Bird Yes, that's all right, but how do you feel now, knowing that these people have been in jail for years?

Fortune Well I feel, I feel absolutely appalled, I must say that I think constantly of the, of the ringleader, John O'Reilly. Well when I say ringleader, I only use that word in the sense that of course he, he actually didn't do anything, and in fact, hadn't met the other two, before they were arrested, but anyway for the . . .

Bird For the purposes of this interview . . .

Fortune Yes, I think about them a great deal, I think about him spending fifteen years of his life in prison, his life wasting away day by day, and I think of the things that he obviously missed.

Bird Yes, it must have been . . .

Fortune Mainly the theatre.

Bird Pardon? The theatre, yes . . .

Fortune Yes. Do you like the theatre at all?

Bird Do I like it? Yes, quite.

Fortune I love the theatre . . .

Bird Do you?

Fortune My wife and I go two or three times a week.

Bird Really?

Fortune Well it's very easy, we live in the Temple, we have a flat there, so we just walk up through the gardens, pop across the Strand, and then it's just up Drury Lane, and one can go and see a wonderful show like *42nd Street.*

Bird You enjoyed that did you?

Fortune Did you see *42nd Street*?

Bird Yes I did, it was terrific wasn't it, absolutely . . .

Fortune Joyous, joyous evening in the theatre.

Bird Yes, wonderful . . .

Fortune That wonderful little girl, um . . .

Bird Oh yes, who was that? Um . . . Bonnie Langford, was it?

Fortune Bonnie Langford, yes.

Bird Yes.

Fortune I believe it . . . was she in *42nd Street*?

Bird I think so, yes.

Fortune I've certainly seen a lot of her. I have a terrible memory for names and faces, and facts of course. But yes, Bonnie Langford, and she actually illustrates a very important point, I think.

Bird Does she?

Fortune I think a lot of people think of Judges as rather remote, callous, detached . . .

Bird Unworldly figures, yes.

Fortune . . . but I actually have to say that if Bonnie Langford appeared before me, in court, on a very very serious matter, grievous bodily harm, something like that, then I would certainly have to declare an interest.

Bird Because you admired her so much in *42nd Street*?

Fortune Absolutely.

Bird I mean it's very unlikely that she would appear on grievous . . .

Fortune I suppose on the face of it it is. But . . .

Bird But . . .

Fortune On the face, it certainly is a fact that John O'Reilly never saw Bonnie Langford in *42nd Street*, if indeed she was in it, because when the show opened he was already in prison . . .

Bird And he was still there when it closed.

Fortune He was still there . . . rather prematurely closed I thought.

Bird What, the show closed prematurely? Yes, I think it did.

Fortune My wife and I were hoping to see it for our seventh time.

Bird But just . . . yes. Just to get off *42nd Street* . . .

Fortune Yes, of course.

Bird For the time being . . .

Fortune Of course.

Bird . . . And back to the case which we are discussing, John O'Reilly . . .

Fortune Absolutely.

Bird . . . I mean he at least felt, I suppose, during that time, the fifteen years, well he felt that he knew he was innocent, so that must have been . . .

Fortune Well that must have been a matter of tremendous consolation to him.

Bird And great strength I should think . . .

Fortune And great strength.

Bird Yes.

Fortune It must have been a very present help in trouble.

Bird Yes, and he . . .

Fortune And of course he didn't feel appalling remorse and guilt, which . . .

Bird Which you do.

Fortune Well, certainly, since this business has come out . . .

Bird Yes. You feel . . .

Fortune Agonized, yes. Sometimes, after a long day in court, I get back home at about half past three in the afternoon, and I find it almost impossible to go to sleep.

Bird You're thinking about . . .

Fortune Thinking about him.

Bird Mr O'Reilly?

Fortune Yes. Luckily not completely impossible.

Bird No, no. But can I ask what general thoughts you have about this? I mean the police told you at the appeal hearing that these people were guilty, and I suppose you have to take their word for it, I mean they *are* policemen aren't they?

Fortune Well this is the great difficulty, you see in the past the judicial system comprised three parts, there were the criminals and then the police and then the judiciary . . .

Bird Like yourself.

Fortune Yes. Well now I'm afraid there are only two parts. That's the problem.

Bird The judiciary, and the police and the criminals have . . .

Fortune Have sort of merged . . . merged together, yes. Which makes it terribly difficult for us.

Bird It makes it terribly difficult, and just handing down long prison sentences doesn't really work because . . .

Fortune Well it means that one has got to take some responsibility.

Bird Yes. And also they spend all this time in prison and they just come out and they start being policemen again. But what, I mean, what is the answer, is there an answer to it?

Fortune Well I think it's very difficult, I think really the only answer is hanging.

Bird Yes. In the sense that if they, they . . .

Fortune Well in the sense that if they're dead, there won't be all these investigations, there wouldn't be any point in it. And also, from the point of view . . .

Bird And they wouldn't miss *42nd Street* either, I suppose.

Fortune That's what I was going to say, from the point of view of Mr O'Reilly, because I mean there are theologians in this country who do believe that there may be an after-life in which theatrical performances of famous musicals may take place.

Bird Although we can't count on that I imagine.

Fortune Well no.

Bird No.

Fortune And I personally can't imagine a more heavenly production of *42nd Street* than the one that I saw . . .

Bird But just to go back to this capital punishment, and hanging . . .

Fortune Yes.

Bird I mean, of course we don't have that, except in an informal way, I mean some people in prison have started . . .

Fortune Yes, it has crept back . . .

Bird On a Do-It-Yourself sort of basis.

Fortune Yes, they've voted with their pyjama cords.

Bird But you don't have much control over that, I mean it's . . .

Fortune No it is rather random.

Bird These people taking the law into their own hands.

Fortune Exactly. And we do feel that if we had got any control over people hanging themselves, then in a sense there isn't a great deal of place for judges.

Bird Yes I suppose so. But it is a rather barbaric procedure, I mean, six o'clock in the morning the Governor comes and taps on the cell door and says; 'Good morning, would you like some kedgeree for breakfast, you're going to be hanged in a minute?' I mean, it's not very nice is it?

Fortune No. Or a sausage or something?

Bird No no, well whatever the breakfast is, really.

Fortune Yes.

Bird I mean I wouldn't pick kedgeree myself, I don't suppose.

Fortune I don't know, I think kedgeree might be a very wise choice.

Bird Oh?

Fortune Yes, I mean provided one could accompany it with half a bottle of very good Chablis.

Bird At six o'clock in the morning, it's rather early isn't it?

Fortune Yes, I generally don't drink that early in the day, because I tend to go to sleep in the afternoon, but on that occasion . . .

Bird	It wouldn't matter too much.
Fortune	No.
Bird	But even so, I mean you're taken out of a cell, six o'clock in the morning, and taken to some dank prison yard . . .
Fortune	Completely barbaric.
Bird	And hanged, very barbaric, I mean what's the answer?
Fortune	Well I suppose something like Trafalgar Square.
Bird	Oh I see, in public . . . ?
Fortune	Make a day of it, you know, a family outing day. I'm sure British Rail would lay on some specials . . .
Bird	Awaydays . . .
Fortune	Awaydays.
Bird	Well Lord Justice Merry, thank you very much for coming along and sharing your thoughts with us.
Fortune	Thank you very much.

NHS

We had done a piece in one of the BBC Bremner shows which took the form of an interview with the chief executive of an NHS Trust who was anxious to 'market' his hospital more effectively, in his case by opening a branch of Next clothing shop in what had been an operating theatre ('Let's put your haemorrhoids on the back burner for a moment, Mr Jenkins: how would you like a new suit?'). Here are excerpts from two more conversations dealing with the Government's belief that the NHS, like everything else, would work better if it was run as a business.

We thought of the conceit of a surgeon putting out a tender for a scalpel as a piece of extreme comic exaggeration, but we were constantly told by people who actually work in the Health Service that it paled beside actual practice. Indeed there was a newspaper story two years later which told of a patient in a Glasgow hospital whose stitches were to be removed following an operation: instead of wasting valuable resources by coming in to have it done she was sent an envelope containing a scalpel and instructions on how to do it herself. A step in the right direction, but surely she could have provided her own scalpel?

1993

Fortune	George Parr, you were recently appointed Chief Executive of the South Herefordshire NHS Healthcare Trust . . .
Bird	That's right, yes.
Fortune	To bring the disciplines of the market into the National Health Service . . .
Bird	Very much so, yes.
Fortune	And so you're in fact responsible for eleven hospitals in your area.
Bird	Two. There were eleven last week, but we've downsized the operation and there are two.
Fortune	I see.
Bird	In the interests of efficiency and slimming down the . . .
Fortune	Well this is what we're going to talk about isn't it?
Bird	Of course, yes.
Fortune	The discipline of the market, was this the first thing you did on taking office?

Bird Well the first thing we did was what our colleagues in private industry do: the senior executives and myself went away to a large country hotel for a week, and brainstormed about our problems, and we took some pretty hard decisions there.

Fortune And this was one of them, to downsize the operation?

Bird Well the first one was to give ourselves very large increases in salary, and then to make a corporate video.

Fortune It is a problem isn't it, because in the National Health Service, as Mrs Thatcher noted a long time ago, demand is infinite, isn't it?

Bird Well, Mrs Bottomley said, and these figures are right, that there is now more demand on the National Health Service than there ever has been, and yet at the same time the nation's health is better than ever. Now, this can only indicate one thing.

Fortune And what is that?

Bird Well that patients aren't really ill. I mean a lot of patients aren't ill.

Fortune They're presenting themselves to hospital without illnesses . . .

Bird	Well yes, I think it's . . . you see the problem is rather like benefits . . .
Fortune	Yes.
Bird	That if people know they're going to get unemployment benefit they are being rewarded for being out of work, and so there's no incentive for them to take work.
Fortune	I understand, yes.
Bird	Now at the same time, if people feel they're going to be rewarded for being ill . . .
Fortune	By treatment . . .
Bird	By being treated, yes, there's no incentive for them not to be ill.
Fortune	Yes.
Bird	And so we're trying to get this question of incentive into it, because that's a market force.
Fortune	So you are going to bring the discipline of the market into the hospital, and if possible extend it?

Bird We're extending it not just to the broad brush, the fact that, you know, that we provide, and fund-holders purchase from us, but inside the very operation of the hospitals themselves, we're going to operate a market system.

Fortune In what sort of way?

Bird Well I'll give you an example; in the old days, before I took over, in the operating theatre you would have a body, a patient on the thing, the table, and the surgeon would want to cut him open he'd say 'scalpel'.

Fortune Yes.

Bird And a nurse would give him a scalpel.

Fortune I've seen that, yes.

Bird With no consideration about whether he needed the scalpel, or how much the scalpel cost, or whether he could get a scalpel cheaper somewhere else, whether indeed he could use an old razor blade he'd brought from home, or . . .

Fortune Paper clips . . .

Bird A paper clip, yes, or even his own teeth, if he had any teeth.

Fortune So what will happen now?

Bird Well, if he does establish that it is necessary, then immediately he will make a bid for a scalpel, he'll put out a bid.

Fortune A tender.

Bird A tender for a scalpel, and he will first of all ask round the operating theatre to see if another nurse has got a scalpel cheaper than the nurse who's standing next to him.

Fortune Which is possible.

Bird It's very unlikely because we only have one nurse in the operating theatre. But then what he will do is to contact our new . . . this is an appointment I've recently made . . . the Scalpel Resource Manager, who I've put in at a salary of £45,000 a year, and he will, as soon as he hears that a scalpel is needed . . .

Fortune Perhaps . . .

Bird Perhaps in operating theatre A . . .

Fortune Yes.

Bird Or . . . well it will be A, we only have one operating theatre, he will immediately go into action and ring round the whole country, send faxes to see where he can lay his hands on the cheapest possible scalpel. And now if that happens to be in Barrow-in-Furness, that's where he'll get it from.

Fortune He will personally go and get it will he?

Bird He will get it. Well, we are talking about emergencies here.

Fortune Well it's not going to be sent by post.

Bird No, no.

Fortune He'll jump in the car . . .

Bird He'll drive up there in his Seven Series BMW, which is what he gets . . .

Fortune With the job?

Bird Yes, absolutely.

Fortune Because otherwise people aren't taken seriously, are they, without those sorts of things. Well that, that sounds very radical. In fact, one might think that in some way you might be able to get rid of the middle-men in this transaction entirely.

Bird Get rid of the doctors you mean, and the surgeons, yes, well we can . . .

Fortune It's a thought.

Bird What we are hoping you see to . . . it is a matter of patient choice . . .

Fortune Yes.

Bird To empower the patients to take their own decisions.

Fortune Yes.

Bird And indeed make their own incisions, if it should be cheaper.

Fortune So the patient would come in . . .

Bird The patient would come in with a growth that he has and say, 'what are you going to do about this growth?' and I would say: 'what are you going to about it?'

Fortune And you would empower him to use the resources of the . . .

Bird Yes, we would lease an operating theatre, a mirror.

Fortune A mirror, of course.

Bird And a book on major surgery and how to do it.

Fortune Yes, and he'd be able to resource himself.

Bird And he'd be able to get on with it. He'd be able to resource himself, yes, he would be able to stand on his own two feet, well perhaps not if he was . . .

Fortune . . . doing something.

Bird Having an anaesthetic, no.

Fortune No. But at the same time it must be admitted that in terms of pure management . . .

Bird Yes.

Fortune Don't the patients get in the way rather?

Bird Well, no, I wouldn't say they got in the way, but you see what we are trying to do is create a buzzing thrusting entrepreneurial business atmosphere in our new hospital and it is perfectly true that this is not very easy, because there's a lot of people lying about being sick, and . . .

Fortune Groaning.

Bird And groaning, so that it is possible that we would get rid of them, as they have done in ICI.

Fortune George Parr, thank you very much indeed.

Bird Thank you, not at all.

1994

Fortune The Government is planning to introduce performance related pay in the National Health Service . . . Sir George Parr, you're a management consultant working for the Department of Health. Thank you very much for coming along to answer a few questions.

Bird Not at all, anything that I can do to illuminate the situation, fire ahead.

Fortune Can I, can I first ask you, why is the Government going to introduce performance related pay in the National Health Service?

[LONG PAUSE]

Bird Do you know, I knew you'd ask that question. I'm sorry, I said to my wife, you know, I hate being asked that question. Um. I've been asked that before, but no I'm sorry, you'll have to ask something else, ha ha, because . . .

Fortune Well if I can, if I can press you on this, I mean there must be a reason isn't there?

Bird Well, I suppose there is, yes, there

must be a reason, yes of course, unless they're doing it for a bet or something like that. But . . .

Fortune But when this scheme is introduced, presumably the managers are going to have to find some criteria for assessing the performance of these people?

Bird Yes, yes, it's got to be simple and it's got to be easily measurable and . . .

Fortune How carefully a doctor looks after his patient, that sort of thing?

Bird Oh no no no no. What it comes down to is what we call Throughput.

Fortune Throughput?

Bird Yes, the number of patients coming in to the hospital, and how quickly they go out again. That is the measure of a hospital's performance, obviously it's good for a hospital to have a lot of patients coming in, and it's very good for them to go out again as quickly as possible. Because patients, by definition, who come into the hospital are ill.

Fortune Yes.

Bird And when they go out they're better.

And the quicker they go out the better they are.

Fortune Yes, so if I follow your logic, the best hospital would be one where a patient arrives in an ambulance and is put on a trolley and rushed through the hospital, through an operating theatre where the doctor will shout: 'There he goes', that sort of thing, someone would write down his name and number, and then he'd be rushed out the back of the hospital, put in an ambulance and taken home.

Bird Do you mind if I write this down?

[TAKES NOTES]

Bird That is . . . that is a very good idea, we could call it the fast-track treatment, couldn't we, that would look rather good in our brochures.

Fortune Doesn't this mean, however, that patient care is going out the window?

Bird That's another very good idea, I'll write that down, it would certainly free the bottlenecks at the doors, yes.

Fortune Yes.

Bird But there are of course other criteria,

apart from that, I mean it's not just numbers we're talking about.

Fortune Well that's very reassuring to hear.

Bird Yes, there are other very important factors in any health environment; costs is the main one.

Fortune Money.

Bird Money, yes.

Fortune I see.

Bird The money will come from savings created by greater efficiency.

Fortune And what does that mean?

Bird Well it means what it always means, which is cutting services and replacing expensive qualified staff by cheap unqualified staff and by firing people you don't like the look of.

Fortune And what result would that have? I mean would that . . .

Bird Well, well one result would be that you would get the creation of many more jobs.

Fortune I'm trying very hard to understand

this point. You sack a lot of doctors, but you create more jobs?

Bird Not doctors, no no, you create jobs for management consultants, like myself, who would be necessary to . . .

Fortune Oh I see, yes.

Bird I mean after all that would save the taxpayer money, because it takes seven years to train a doctor, but you can learn to be a management consultant in one weekend at the Chewton Glen Hotel.

Fortune Sir George Parr, thank you very much indeed.

LADY PAMELA

Performed on 18 November 1994. It was one of those weeks when some Conservative Minister (we don't remember which, they all seemed to merge into each other at the time) forced his wife and family to pose at their front door for press photographers to demonstrate that they were 'standing by him'.

What you have to keep in mind while reading this piece is that John Fortune appeared as he normally does: a middle-aged man in a dark grey suit.

Bird We've had a lot of discussion, this week particularly, about wives' loyalty to their husbands, and particularly the wives of Conservative MPs. We tend to assume sometimes that these women are the mere appendages as it were of their husbands . . .

Fortune Quite.

Bird . . . of their husbands' careers, and we don't get the woman's point of view. Lady Pamela Parr, you are the wife of a junior minister in the Conservative government, who's over the years had a . . . been involved in a number of incidents, controversial incidents.

Fortune Unfortunately, yes.

Bird Yes. And now er . . . I don't think that you would think of yourself as just a wife, would you?

Fortune No, I hope I'm rather more than that.

Bird I mean you have had a career of your own . . .

Fortune Certainly.

Bird . . . you've been active in the Women's Institute . . .

Fortune Yes, yes.

Bird You were a past Chairman of the Conservative Women's National Committee, and the past President . . .

Fortune Yes. I do think it's very vital for every woman to have her own identity.

Bird Hmmm, yes.

Fortune But having said that, I am of course first and foremost a political wife.

Bird Yes, um . . .

Fortune And that's a twenty-four-hour job, I don't mind telling you . . .

Bird Yes, I'm sure it is, yes . . .

Fortune I mean really.

Bird I'm sure it is.

Fortune I don't have any time of my own. I could be woken up at four in the morning by Sir George coming home and banging about in the kitchen.

Bird Yes.

Fortune Or the *News of the World* pounding on the front door and demanding an interview.

Bird Yes. And you've had experience of that quite a lot haven't you, recently, because your husband was involved some time ago with his research assistant, and recently I think with a Lebanese lady . . .

Fortune A Lebanese lady was the latest.

Bird But you very publicly stood by him.

Fortune Yes I have, because I think it's my

duty, as a wife and a mother.

[LONG PAUSE]

Bird Yes. Um. Lady Pamela, I hope you don't mind if I ask a rather personal question?

Fortune Go ahead, please.

Bird Well, it's just that, that that um, you present, how can I put this, a rather masculine appearance.

Fortune You noticed.

Bird Yes.

Fortune Yes, well several months ago I underwent a procedure, by which my . . . my gender was changed.

Bird You had a sex change operation?

Fortune Yes, in popular parlance, that's . . .

Bird Well I must say it's been terribly successful.

Fortune Thank you very much indeed.

Bird As far as I can tell from this distance, which is the closest I'm going to come.

Fortune Yes.

Bird The question which presents itself is why you had this done?

Fortune Why? Well I had the first inklings of this, of this decision some time last spring, when I was standing on the doorstep of our London house at half past six in the morning, with George and the children, and my parents . . .

Bird Yes.

Fortune . . . and having our photograph taken . . .

Bird This was the usual routine thing of . . .

Fortune A show of unity.

Bird A show of unity by the family . . .

Fortune Yes, and I was holding his hand and laying my head on his shoulder and gazing up at him, adoringly. And then a thought struck me.

Bird You thought: you couldn't take this any more?

Fortune No. No no, not at all. What I thought was: is this actually helpful?

Bird Yes. I see. Yes.

Fortune Because there I was in my little pink dress and high heeled shoes and I'd been up all night getting my hair right and all that sort of thing, and then I suddenly thought people seeing the photographs or me on television, what are they going to be thinking?

Bird Indeed.

Fortune They're going to be thinking; there's the little wife, down-trodden woman . . .

Bird Yes.

Fortune Betrayed yet again . . .

Bird By a monster . . .

Fortune By a monster.

Bird Yes.

Fortune And waves of sympathy would come in my direction.

Bird Their hearts would go out to you.

Fortune Instead of their hearts going out to George.

Bird	Yes, it's the Judith Mellor syndrome really, isn't it, I mean . . .
Fortune	Absolutely, absolutely. After all George is the Minister, and everyone's terribly terribly sorry for Judith, who's got a heart as big as a bus.
Bird	Yes.
Fortune	But on the other hand, people are also thinking that David Mellor is an appalling, ghastly person, and that isn't the object of the exercise.
Bird	It's very much counter-productive isn't it?
Fortune	Absolutely.
Bird	So they . . . you might think that if people saw that instead of the normal picture of a husband with a little woman, as it were, by his side, er if there were . . .
Fortune	There would be two chaps.
Bird	. . . two men, exactly. Fellows. And they would be able to assess the situation rather more objectively.
Fortune	There would be, yes, there would be two chaps standing there, rather like,

you know, two chaps going out to bat for England.

Bird Yes. Except they wouldn't be holding hands would they?

Fortune Well not at Lords.

Bird No.

Fortune And of course in the future I won't be holding George's hand, because I think that would be very tasteless.

Bird Of course, yes. I see that, but you don't think that this tableau, as it were, of two men standing by the children and the in-laws, wouldn't *that* be rather embarrassing and curious?

Fortune Oh not at all, not at all, because people would think you see that it would be all right for George to have affairs with other women as long as he was married to a man.

Bird Yes.

Fortune You do see the logic of that?

Bird Yes, yes yes. I, I . . .

Fortune Because there wouldn't be that

tension between the wife and the mistress.

Bird No, I do see that. And of course, when Judith Mellor says she understands, people don't believe her, do they?

Fortune Of course they don't.

Bird I mean they they think how could she possibly? But you, I mean . . .

Fortune Well I, I could understand because I'm a man.

Bird Yes . . .

Fortune But I really am a man, I'm not just dressed up as a man, I promise you that . . .

Bird Yes, I very very much take your word for that.

Fortune And also as as a man I can see the kind of temptations that might lie in wait for a minister of the Crown.

Bird Yes.

Fortune Because there's, there's honestly a great deal more to George than just sex scandals.

Bird Is there? What?

Fortune Well there's corruption for a start.

Bird Yes?

Fortune I mean you mentioned the Lebanese lady a little while ago . . .

Bird Yes.

Fortune . . . and I can perfectly understand how that could happen, because George was involved in these high level negotiations with a Middle Eastern country about arms sales. And therefore he was bound, sooner or later, to become entangled, however briefly, with this, with this young lady.

Bird Yes, but she wasn't actually negotiating . . .

Fortune She wasn't actually on the negotiating team.

Bird She was a belly-dancer wasn't she?

Fortune Yes. Yes she was, she came springing out of a cake, in the shape of an armoured personnel carrier . . . and was sort of thrust in George's face more or less.

Bird	Yes.
Fortune	So I can understand that.
Bird	Going back to your own situation, if we may, people might think that you had taken this, that you'd cut off this . . .
Fortune	My past.
Bird	Your past, yes, taken this radical step, to fulfil some sort of emotional need of your own.
Fortune	Oh no, that's completely wrong.
Bird	A cry for help.
Fortune	No no no. It wasn't a personal thing.
Bird	Well it seems fairly personal to me.
Fortune	No I, what I did I did for my husband, for my party, and for my country, call me old-fashioned if you like, but I'm an old-fashioned girl.
Bird	Yes. Or man.
Fortune	Or man, yes. And I think it would be a tremendous tragedy if this Government fell, rather like the Macmillan Government, because of a

number of sex scandals, because this Government has still got an enormous amount to offer, in terms of policy, in terms of upholding family values.

Bird So in a way this is the ultimate sacrifice that you've made, isn't it?

Fortune Well no, I think there are far worse things than what I've done. Have you been very close to George?

Bird No, no, I must say I haven't, but you have.

Fortune Well I suppose there was an element of sacrifice in it, but as my surgeon said, when I was under the knife; just lie back and think of England.

Bird Yes, your husband was a very lucky man to to have such a loyal partner . . .

Fortune Thank you.

Bird . . . And what has he said to you about this, what does he think?

Fortune I've no idea, he hasn't noticed.

Bird Really?

Fortune But then he is a very busy man.

Bird Lady, Lady Pamela, thank you very much.

YOUTH CRIME

The Criminal Justice and Public Order Bill 1994 introduced new sentencing powers for courts to pass a 'secure training order', under which juveniles aged 12 to 14 would be detained in five specially built secure institutions for up to two years. Many bodies had submitted advice to the Home Secretary on the wisdom of this idea, including specialists from the Home Office itself. Most of the advice echoed the sentiments of an editorial in the journal of the Magistrates' Association of February 1993:

> 'The belief that school age offenders who persist in committing offences can be reformed into law abiding citizens, if removed from their damaging home circumstances and given education in a secure environment, is not new. . . . The reality is that, attractive as the idea may be, there is abundant evidence available from the recent past that it does not work . . . it is horrendously expensive and wasteful of funds demonstrably better spent elsewhere in the juvenile system. . . .
>
> 'Please, Home Secretary, consider funding community-based programmes which have a track record of success rather than throwing our money, and at the same time your reputation as a penal policy-maker, down a drain which can only lead to expensive failure.'

When Michael Howard reads stuff like that his response is certain: 'Magistrates! Trendy left-wing so-called experts! What do they know? Let's do it!'

Bird We've seen this week that people are still very concerned about teenage thuggery, juvenile yobs and . . .

Fortune Gangsters.

Bird Gangsters, yes, but it's not just Young Conservatives that people are worried about, it's the whole idea of teenage crime. Now George Parr, you are the Director of the Penal Policy Research . . .

Fortune Institute, yes.

Bird And you've been advising Michael Howard, the Home Secretary, on punishment for youth crime . . . and I gather that you have suggested, and he is putting into the Criminal Justice Bill, in fact it's going to be next year they're going to start . . .

Fortune That's right.

Bird . . . these prisons; what are they called, Secure Training Units?

Fortune Secure Training Units, yes.

Bird For under-fourteens.

Fortune Under fourteen-year-olds.

Bird Now are you connected, is your Institute connected with the Conservative Party?

Fortune Oh by no means, we're completely independent.

Bird Oh right.

Fortune We enjoy some funding from an American company that's been long experienced in the field of the private administration of child prisons.

Bird Yes.

Fortune 'Chains R Us'. And they've been tremendously helpful, but we're completely politically neutral.

Bird But this is an argument really isn't it between, as it were, care and punishment?

Fortune Absolutely . . .

Bird I mean care on the one hand, meaning nurturing . . .

Fortune Meaning rehabilitation and some kind

of psychotherapeutic method of making children better.

Bird And punishment on the other hand meaning . . .

Fortune Meaning punishment.

Bird And can you just outline these plans?

Fortune Well, as Mr Howard has said, policy in this area has been in the hands for far too long of the kind of woolly-minded, do-gooding minority.

Bird Yes.

Fortune And it's time we had a change in that.

Bird Yes, yes.

Fortune So . . .

Bird You're not a do-gooder?

Fortune No, certainly not.

Bird You're a do-badder are you?

Fortune Well in that sense, yes.

Bird And is this entirely just an academic viewpoint that you have?

The many faces of John Bird and John Fortune.

Here are two of them.

Here are some more.

Own clothes.

With the benefit of wardrobe.

An action sequence...

...continued.

Don’t try this at home

Spot the Dog.

Which puppy belongs to which John?

(See the following page)

The Office

(Top dog: Phoebe (a Saluki) John Fortune
Bottom dog: Zebedee (a Briard) John Bird)

Fortune Not at all, because young people committing appalling offenses up and down the land touches us all.

Bird Yes, well I can see you're touched.

Fortune I am touched.

Bird So you're personally affected are you?

Fortune Yes, and I've had terrible personal experience in this area . . .

Bird Really?

Fortune Yes. My son, Toby, was sent to a secure unit.

Bird Really. Really? And did he benefit from this?

Fortune Not at all, no. He was forced to mix with the dregs of society; violence, drug-taking, homosexuality, and so we decided in the end to take him out of Harrow . . .

Bird I see.

Fortune And he's gone to work on his own.

Bird Yes.

Fortune Although, of course, sending him to

Harrow was a great deal cheaper than sending him to prison.

Bird The fees are less, are they?

Fortune Much less. But on the other hand when you leave prison you're not automatically offered a job in the City.

Bird No. Not unless you had a job in the City before you went to prison.

Fortune That's true.

Bird But there is a school of thought, which you regard as woolly-minded, which would suggest that the way to deal with these young people is actually for them to be nurtured properly, parented properly . . .

Fortune From a very early age.

Bird . . . In the first few months of their life, first year of their life.

Fortune Well I think that's ridiculous don't you? I mean have you, have you ever met a victim of a mugging by a six-month-old baby?

Bird No. What we . . .

Fortune I mean what we . . . Honestly, I'm sorry . . .

Bird What I'm suggesting is that . . . it might prevent them becoming criminals later on.

Fortune No no no no, we live in the real world, let's call a spade a spade. These young people are no better than animals. And as such they should be treated like animals.

Bird Yes.

Fortune I mean let me give you an illustration. If you're in the jungle say, and a lion jumps out on you, I mean what are you going to do? Are you going to say: 'Why not go somewhere on safari?'

Bird Well no, you wouldn't say that, well you're already . . .

Fortune He is already on safari. Or would you say: 'Listen lion, let's sit down and talk about your early childhood, did your lioness mother parent you badly as a little cub?'

Bird No, you wouldn't say that.

Fortune You'd be mad to say that. No what you do is you take your rifle and you shoot him.

Bird Yes. Yes, I see that.

Fortune Through the eyes.

Bird Yes, of course, and afterwards what would happen, I mean . . . ?

Fortune Well then the lion can be turned into some socially acceptable and even decorative object, like a rug.

Bird Yes . . .

Fortune In front of the fire.

Bird I don't think we can push this analogy too far can we? I mean there are very few people who would want the skin of some pimply adolescent with his tattoos and hypodermic needle marks stretched out in front of their blazing logs.

Fortune Well I certainly wouldn't.

Bird Neither would I. But in fact you're saying that by the time these children get to sort of sixteen years old it's too late to deal with them in a humane way . . .

Fortune Much too late, and who's to blame for that? I mean honestly, it can't be a coincidence, can it, that these fifteen- and sixteen-year-olds have had fifteen or sixteen years since the last Labour Government?

Bird Yes, I see what you're . . .

Fortune I mean if anybody was going to do something about it . . .

Bird I understand that, can we just get onto these secure training units . . .

Fortune Yes, of course, of course.

Bird . . . that are going to be set up. The first one is going to be opened next year.

Fortune Yes.

Bird There are going to be five of them I understand.

Fortune There are going to be five, yes.

Bird And how many young people are going to be in them?

Fortune There are going to be forty young people under the age of fourteen . . .

Bird Forty . . .

Fortune . . . in each of the five units.

Bird Yes, so there are going to be in other

words two hundred young people throughout the whole country.

Fortune Two hundred of the very worst children in the land.

Bird Yes. Of course there already are residential units, operated by local authorities . . .

Fortune That's right.

Bird And they cost around, I think the maximum is about £39,000 per inmate . . .

Fortune Quite, per year.

Bird What about your secure units?

Fortune Well the cost in the secure training units for each individual will be £150,000 a year.

Bird £150,000 a year . . .

Fortune Yes.

Bird . . . for each one.

Fortune For each one.

Bird And you'll have two hundred.

Fortune That's right.

Bird Now the last statistics we had was that the number of children under fourteen who have been convicted or cautioned for indictable offenses was I think 32,200.

Fortune 32,200, yes.

Bird And you'll be dealing with two hundred of them, so there'll be, at a rough estimate, 32,000, as it were.

Fortune That we haven't . . .

Bird It means that you have to choose the right two hundred don't you, to put inside?

Fortune Well that's absolutely vital, yes, we must be sure.

Bird I mean these are going to be really the most persistent . . .

Fortune . . . the really worst.

Bird . . . the really nastiest, and most violent . . .

Fortune Absolutely.

Bird . . . and how are you going to select them?

Fortune Well I think it's going to be self-selecting isn't it? I mean it's going to be such a social piece of prestige for these two hundred people to think they are . . .

Bird They're going to think they're the worst possible young people . . .

Fortune They are the worst, the very hardest worst cases.

Bird So they'll *want* to get in there will they?

Fortune They'll be fighting to get in, of course they will.

Bird It would be great peer group prestige for them . . .

Fortune Absolutely. Even a waiting list.

Bird Like the MCC.

Fortune Very much like the MCC, yes. With a different sort of tie of course.

Bird The other thing of course is that from experience that we've had of having young people in custody, it does affect some of them very badly.

Fortune Yes.

Bird I mean we've had nineteen, I think in one year, nineteen suicides amongst young people who've been kept in custody.

Fortune Well that's a start isn't it. It's also proof, if proof were needed, that this type of austere regime really works.

Bird Yes, and of course if there are nineteen that do commit suicide that would save you quite a lot of money at a hundred and fifty thousand pounds, that would save you three million pounds.

Fortune Of taxpayers' money.

Bird Exactly. And of course there'd be nine-teen places left open now for . . .

Fortune For the second division to move up.

Bird To move up. And if this doesn't work, I mean it's fairly unlikely, but if it doesn't work, do you have any other policies?

Fortune Well there are some more radical plans. We're thinking of adopting some ideas from our colleagues in Brazil.

Bird Are you?

Fortune There's a very interesting Institute of Social Policy in Rio de Janeiro; the

Black Hand Death Squad Institute. They've done a very interesting and illuminating study of the proportion of young people between the ages of ten and fourteen who re-offend after they've been shot.

Bird And what results have they . . . ?

Fortune It's very encouraging: very very few.

Bird Is it? Very few.

Fortune Almost none of these young people re-offend after they've been shot dead.

Bird But you're not suggesting that our police should go around shooting . . .

Fortune Oh absolutely not, that's out of the question, no I think it's absolutely essential that we keep this in the private sector.

Bird Yes. So you will have private firms going round shooting . . .

Fortune . . . private firms, because part of the peace dividend in Northern Ireland means that soon there is going to be an enormous number of people who are extremely well-versed and experienced in violence . . .

Bird Shooting people . . .

Fortune Yes, who will be on the labour market.

Bird . . . the IRA and the Ulster . . .

Fortune I was thinking more of the SAS and the Parachute Regiment . . .

Bird Well that's very interesting, thank you very much George Parr for coming to share your thoughts with us.

Fortune Thank you.

THE ARMY

Following the transmission of this piece a large number of calls were made to the Channel 4 Duty Office. Most of the callers, including a man who claimed to be an MP, seemed to be under the impression that the object of our attack was the Danish tour guide who was raped and killed by the three British soldiers on Cyprus who had been given life sentences a few days earlier. (The MP thought she was Swedish.) One gay caller thought it was an attack on homosexuals. Another person was of the opinion that we had libelled the three soldiers by saying they had murdered the girl whereas they had actually been found guilty of manslaughter (and rape). A man who said he was a barrister complained that it was in 'terrible taste' that we should mention a girl who had been beaten to death. We felt that it was rather the beating itself that left something to be desired in the matter of taste, to put it at its mildest.

We sometimes wonder what it is that some people think they have been watching. Indeed, one anonymous complainant said he'd been watching Channel 4 all that evening and was protesting that the Rory Bremner show hadn't gone out at all.

We leave it to the reader to make a judgement about what our attitude on the subject actually was.

Fortune Major General Sir George Parr, you're a senior official at the Ministry of Defence . . .

Bird Yes.

Fortune And the British Army is currently going through a very difficult period isn't it?

Bird Is it?

Fortune Well, for example, the conviction of three British soldiers in Cyprus last week for the murder of a young woman by battering her to death with a spade . . .

Bird Oh, yes.

Fortune The Deputy Commander in Cyprus, Brigadier Arthur Denaro, said that we should put this incident into perspective. What do you think he meant by that?

Bird It's difficult to know really, isn't it? I suppose he must have meant that there are three quarters of a million people living in Cyprus and we only killed one of them. So, you know, it's not a bad proportion really, is it?

Fortune No, but the Cypriots were very upset.

Bird Oh well, we didn't kill a Cypriot, I

mean she wasn't Cypriot was she? She was . . .

Fortune No, she was Danish.

Bird Danish, that's right. I knew it was something like that. And of course what the Brigadier also said which I think was quite true: we must remember that it was these three individual men who were on trial, not the British Army, and certainly not their glorious regiment, the Royal Green Jackets, or the Royal Green Jackets with big red splodges on as they're now called.

Fortune But this is the sort of thing that the Army always says after such an incident, isn't it? You just close ranks and protect your own.

Bird Oh well, I should say that these three men have nothing whatever to do with the Army.

Fortune Oh, in what sense?

Bird Well in the sense that there is a rule in the Army, and a very good one I think, that you are immediately dismissed from the Army as soon as you murder somebody. Well unless you're doing it as part of your work of course. And also, there is this question you see . . . you're getting a whole big group of fit young men, who are all together, miles from home, nothing to do but drink and lie in the sun all day, and you are bound to get these occasional outbursts of high spirits.

Fortune Violence.

Bird Well, all right, violence, yes.

Fortune Extreme violence.

Bird Well yes, all right, extreme violence.

Fortune Murdering.

Bird All right, murdering, yes! But, I mean, you don't have to go to Cyprus for that, you get it in every town and city up and down Britain every weekend, every Saturday night you get groups of young men, who are just getting drunk, hanging around and attacking innocent passers-by. There's something wrong with our society. Bring back National Service, that's what I say. You know, couple of years in the Army, that'll soon sort these people out.

Fortune But these people *were* in the Army.

Bird Well yes, that's true.

Fortune And the fact is that some of the most dangerous towns in Britain are those towns which have Army barracks, like Aldershot. Where ordinary people simply can't go into the city on a Saturday night.

Bird Well, who wants to go into Aldershot on a Saturday night? And in any case, the Army are doing their best, they're taking these young men out and sending them abroad and letting them loose on foreigners, which of course is exactly what the Army does. I mean that's its point . . .

Fortune That's its core business, in a sense.

Bird That's right.

Fortune But, but this is the problem isn't it, with a professional army in peace-time . . .

Bird Yes.

Fortune . . . I mean the men that were heroes when they were fighting in the Falklands or in the Gulf are the very same men that you'd run a mile from if you met them in a pub on a Saturday night.

Bird Well, this is what we're faced with as a paradox. I mean if you were set on by a lout with a broken bottle, who would you want to come to your defence? Would you want some sensitive, liberal, *Guardian*-reading person who comes along and says, you know, let's sit down and talk about this? Or do you want a bigger lout with a bigger broken bottle? That's what you want.

Fortune Tell me, is this the thinking behind not wanting homosexual men and women in the armed forces?

Bird Sorry, what do you mean, 'thinking'?

Fortune Well, I mean, the assumption that homosexuals are somehow more sensitive and more liberal-minded than others.

Bird I think that's a rather crude stereotype, isn't it, really?

Fortune Then why don't you want them in the armed forces?

Bird We don't like them.

Fortune And how do you know that you don't like them . . . ?

Bird Because . . . because we had a survey.

Fortune Oh really?

Bird We surveyed the armed forces, and we took a random sample of opinion.

Fortune Asked them what sort of questions, for example?

Bird Well, we asked scientifically rational questions.

Fortune Uh huh.

Bird And one of them was; 'Do you find male homosexuality and female homosexuality equally abhorrent? Do you find one more disgusting than another?' I mean that sort of thing.

Fortune And what sort of replies did you get?

Bird Well, we studied the replies very carefully, and and we thought on the whole that it came down less than positive to . . . well I can give you an actual example of a reply: 'I would quite happily smash their faces in if I found any in my unit.' And we, we took that as being, on the whole, . . .

Fortune At least ambiguous.

Bird Ambiguous, yes. Or at least slightly negative, obviously.

Fortune Yes. So a whole range of questions was asked . . .

Bird We asked, we asked certain questions concerning actual situations in army life . . .

Fortune Such as?

Bird Well, if you're asleep at night in your barracks in your bed would you want, er, suddenly to be woken up in the middle of the night by a limp-wristed, perfumed person with heavy make-up, clambering on top of you, putting their their sexual organ into your bottom?

Fortune What was the reply?

Bird Eighty-six percent said 'Yes' but we assumed they had misunderstood the question.

Fortune Yes, I . . . Of course, there is a parallel here, isn't there, with the problem of racism, because only last week the Commission for Racial Equality came down very hard on the Ministry of Defence . . .

Bird Hmmm.

Fortune . . . for the treatment of blacks in the Army, of both physical and verbal abuse . . .

Bird Well . . .

Fortune I mean people being called 'coons' and 'black bastards', that sort of thing.

Bird Sorry, you said 'abuse'. Where's the . . . ?

Fortune Well if you were black, I think that might be thought of as abusive.

Bird Well I suppose if you are looking for nuances . . . or if you're particularly hypersensitive, yes, I suppose you might think that, yes.

Fortune Hmmm.

Bird But you know, I don't think . . . it's just affectionate banter really, isn't it? I mean, I've been called 'Squiffy' all my life, and it's never worried me very much.

Fortune But, have you ever been put naked into a bath full of urine, and scrubbed with a yard brush?

Bird You'll have to let me think about that for a minute. Um, well, no, not recently, although if you do know a place where I can get that done, I'd be . . . if you could give me the address, the place I usually use has been closed down by the police.

Fortune But it just seems to me you see, in a sense it's obvious that the Army dislikes blacks just as much as it dislikes homosexuals. Why don't you just have a survey about that, and get the answer you want, and then kick the blacks out?

Bird Well, because we can't do that, for various reasons, one is racism is against the law, and also they're not entirely equivalent, the two . . . the two groups of people. After all, um, homosexuals have certain characteristics . . . which don't necessarily present themselves, as it were, on first meeting.

Fortune People can disguise their . . .

Bird I mean we could, for example, operate the policy – we don't want to, but we could – that the American army uses about homosexuals, which is called 'Don't ask, don't tell'.

Fortune Uh huh.

Bird You can't do that so easily with with black people, you see, that's the problem.

Fortune No, that would present certain difficulties.

Bird Black people have certain characteristics. If I can quote again – you may have read this in the newspaper – from a colleague of mine at the Ministry of Defence, Squadron Leader Tony Cowan . . . who said, and I quote: 'Your Afro-Caribbean is a big chap.'

Fortune That's . . .

Bird You see that's rather flattering, I think.

Fortune Yes. Complimentary.

Bird Very, I mean it at least shows there's no racism in the RAF, thank God. 'He's a big chap, often very athletic, and more interested in sport and music.' Well now, you see, that is entirely true, but . . . they are not the *only* characteristics of a black person, those things. I mean, you don't have to wait, for example, before one day in the showers you notice this big fellow jumping up and down singing 'Nobody Knows De Trouble I've Seen', before you realise the sort of chap he is, you see.

Fortune Yes.

Bird Because you have realised that earlier through other indications.

Fortune Yes, the fact that he's black.

Bird The fact that he's black is one of them, yes.

Fortune Yes. This is about trust, isn't it, essentially?

Bird I think it is, it's very much about what Michael Portillo said, when he was announcing the result of this survey about homosexuality: the Army needs trust . . . The people in the Army, they need to trust their mates, and they . . . the thing about homosexuals is you can't trust them, you see, because as, um, as Mr Portillo said, the people in the Army are living literally on top of each other. That is the actual phrase he used, but you can imagine a battlefield situation in today's hi-tech army where a man might be trying to to launch some smart surface-to-air missile . . .

Fortune Ah, yes . . .

Bird And he must absolutely count on the fact that, as he's working out the co-ordinates to the target, there isn't a man standing behind him who is grappling with his trousers. Because, in that case the smart missile could go anywhere.

Fortune Yes, I can see that, but by endorsing these attitudes of your soldiers, aren't you somehow justifying both racism and homophobia?

Bird Oh, no no, we have to protect, we have to stand up for our chaps, because we ask our servicemen to do things on our behalf as a society, that we don't ask anybody else to do.

Fortune Such as?

Bird Kill people.

Fortune Danish tour guides?

Bird Oh no. No, that's just recreational. No, in their actual work we ask them to kill the enemies of our society.

Fortune I see. Well in that case, if society is being defended by the Army, shouldn't the Army reflect the ethnic diversity of this society? I mean, this after all is the argument for having black police officers isn't it?

Bird Well no, the police and the Army are two different things, you see the police work directly with members of the public, the Army doesn't. And we don't ask the police to kill people. I mean they do kill people, but only inadvertently, and then, curiously enough, mainly blacks, but we don't ask them to do that as a matter of course.

Fortune No.

Bird And in any case, I think the Army does reflect society, I mean you would say British society was homophobic and racist, wouldn't you?

Fortune Yes I would.

Bird Well there you are then.

Fortune General Parr, thank you very much indeed.

ASYLUM/IMMIGRATION

'I am proud of this country's record on race relations. But good race relations and firm immigration control go hand in hand. One thing should be understood. Nothing we do to control immigration will be racist. Anyone lawfully in this country will have nothing to fear.

'And let me make one thing absolutely clear. Our immigration policy will be decided here in Britain. And not in Brussels.'

Michael Howard to the Conservative Party Conference 12 October 1995

Bird George Parr, you are a senior political advisor at 10 Downing Street, and I'd like to talk about the Government's policy on asylum and immigration.

Fortune Now, just let me stop you there. Is there anything else you want to talk about?

Bird No, is there a problem here?

Fortune No, it's just that when you say the words immigration and asylum, everyone jumps to the conclusion that the Government just wants to make it more and more difficult for black people to enter this country.

Bird Of course I realise that it's not quite as simple as that.

Fortune Yes it is. But we don't want to give that impression.

Bird Mr Lilley has announced measures to restrict benefit to asylum seekers and Mr Howard has announced a whole new asylum and immigration bill, which will come up in the Queen's speech.

Fortune Yes, and part of that bill will be to announce a list of countries from which applications for political asylum will not be entertained.

Bird The so called white list . . .

Fortune That's right. This will be a list of countries that we regard as being so safe, and so nice to live in that people would be out of their minds to want to leave it.

Bird What, like New Zealand, or somewhere like that?

Fortune Yes, yes.

Bird The curious thing is that the rumours have been that actually three of the countries on the list would be Nigeria . . .

Fortune Nigeria.

Bird . . . Sri Lanka . . .

Fortune Sri Lanka.

Bird . . . and possibly Algeria.

Fortune Algeria, yes.

Bird Yes, and not New Zealand. I mean, why isn't New Zealand on the list?

Fortune Well it would be pointless, wouldn't it, because as far as I know there's never been an application for political asylum from . . .

Bird New Zealand, no . . .

Fortune . . . New Zealand.

Bird On the other hand, last year, there were 7,685 applications from the three countries I mentioned.

Fortune Yes.

Bird And the Home Office is in effect

saying that these three countries are as safe as New Zealand?

Fortune Yes, it's very odd.

Bird Yes.

Fortune It's curious.

Bird It's curious, yes.

Fortune But then again, at the policy unit at Number 10, we do have a saying.

Bird You have a saying do you, what is it?

Fortune It takes all sorts to make a world.

Bird Right. Well, that's given me something to think about. But isn't there a chance that this may appear to be discriminatory against people from these three countries, Nigeria and Sri Lanka and Algeria?

Fortune Absolutely not.

Bird Oh sorry.

Fortune No no no no. No no. It shouldn't be thought in any way that this is a black list.

Bird No.

Fortune	I mean that's why we called it a white list.
Bird	Yes.
Fortune	If we called it a black list there might be certain overtones . . .
Bird	Racial overtones, yes.
Fortune	. . . of race, but in any case, Algerians aren't black are they?
Bird	They're not black, no.
Fortune	But then one could hardly call it the Swarthy with the Big Bushy Moustache list.
Bird	No. So, Peter Lilley is not going to take away all the benefits, is he . . .
Fortune	No no.
Bird	. . . from asylum seekers?
Fortune	No, asylum seekers will get some benefit from the moment when they arrive, to the moment when their application is refused by the Department of Immigration.
Bird	Yes.

Fortune And then of course after that . . .

Bird They can appeal.

Fortune . . . they can appeal. And usually the appeal takes sort of eighteen months, that sort of time.

Bird Yes.

Fortune In which time of course they don't get any benefit.

Bird They don't get any benefit, and they're not allowed to work.

Fortune No, they're not allowed to work.

Bird Which makes it rather difficult then for them to pursue their appeal, I mean they've got no money to spend on legal fees or kebabs, or whatever it is that they eat.

Fortune Well they should have thought of that before, shouldn't they?

Bird Yes . . .

Fortune They should have provided themselves with kebabs or whatever . . .

Bird Kebabs, yes, on their way over. Because they can, and in fact you are encouraging them to pursue their appeals from the country which they left.

Fortune Absolutely, they don't have to appeal from within this country.

Bird No. So somebody who has come out of a prison in Nigeria and has got over here, and has applied for political asylum, and has been turned down . . .

Fortune They're perfectly free to go back to Nigeria.

Bird . . . they can go back to the hell-hole which they left . . .

Fortune Yes.

Bird . . . where they'll be welcomed with open arms of course . . .

Fortune Yes. And they can proceed with their appeals from within, in this case Nigeria. And of course this is the acid test, because if we don't hear from them again . . .

Bird Yes.

Fortune This automatically means that they've changed their minds about political asylum.

Bird And that they think Nigeria is a really good place to live.

Fortune A land flowing with milk and bananas.

Bird Or of course they could be dead.

Fortune Yes, but either way it's a saving to the taxpayer isn't it?

Bird That's perfectly true. But in a Lagos prison cell they're still allowed to write to the Home Secretary.

Fortune Oh yes.

Bird Saying, 'Dear Home Secretary, please excuse the wobbly writing, but the cigarette ends attached to the genitals are making my normal copperplate rather difficult to sustain.' Something like that. But if I could just go on, Michael Howard himself, at the Tory party conference said, and I think I'm quoting from him here, he said: 'nothing we do to control immigration will be racist'.

Fortune That's right.

Bird Hmm. But isn't there a danger that this might appear racist?

Fortune No no, because, in the same speech he said that Britain should be proud of its record on race relations, and good race relations should go hand in hand with a firm immigration policy.

Bird So in other words he means that the fewer people who are let in who are . . . who are, I'm looking for a euphemism for dark-skinned here . . . I'll just call it a euphemism.

Fortune Well, a euphemism, yes.

Bird The fewer euphemisms . . .

Fortune Yes. The fewer euphemisms . . .

Bird The fewer euphemisms who are let in, by definition the fewer potential victims of racial violence there will be.

Fortune Prevention is better than cure isn't it?

Bird So this in fact is really an anti-racist policy.

Fortune It's an anti-racist policy by a Government which is by no means racist, I mean no one could accuse the Prime Minister of being a racist.

Bird No.

Fortune Or Michael Howard.

Bird Certainly not, no.

Fortune Certainly not.

Bird After all, no, his grandparents were Lithuanian[1] immigrants.

Fortune But they weren't black were they? Not that that makes any . . .

Bird Not that that makes any difference . . .

Fortune . . . difference at all.

Bird . . . at all, no. No. So . . .

Fortune So what you're, what you're probably wondering is that if, if the basis of this policy isn't racism . . .

Bird . . . and you're not going to save all that amount of money . . .

Fortune No . . .

Bird . . . then, what is the basis?

Fortune Well the basis of the policy is that the

[1] In the broadcast version we referred to Michael Howard's grandparents as being Lithuanian. This is a mistake: they were in fact Romanian. We apologise to Lithuania.

Prime Minister believes that there are enough racist bigots in the country to swing the next general election, I mean that's democracy isn't it?

Bird Absolutely. And Mr Andrew Lansley, who was until I think this month the Director of Research at Conservative Central Office . . .

Fortune Yes.

Bird . . . wrote an article in September in which he did say that immigration was used successfully by the Conservatives in the 1992 general election, and to use his own phrase 'played well in the tabloids'.

Fortune Yes, what we think is that there are enough *Sun* readers who have been used to voting for the Conservatives, who've bought their own council houses and are having a really really tough time at the moment . . .

Bird Hard time, yes.

Fortune And they don't want things to get worse by having lots of black people come into this country and take the poorly paid part-time jobs that their wives are entitled to.

Bird Yes, exactly. So you think this is the right policy, do you?

Fortune Oh yes it is, absolutely. It's our idea, well it isn't our idea in fact.

Bird Oh really, who's idea is it?

Fortune No, in fact, it's a European idea.

Bird Is it?

Fortune Yes, there was a meeting on the 23rd September last, when the Council of Justice Ministers met and Mr Howard was very highly pressured to adopt these immigration measures, especially the idea of a list of safe countries.

Bird So this is under pressure from Europe, is it?

Fortune Yes.

Bird I don't understand why the Government haven't stressed that point, after all it would take away some of the opprobrium which might mistakenly . . .

Fortune Yes, but the Home Secretary couldn't stand up in front of the Tory conference and say this may be our immigration policy, but really it's all the idea of Brussels.

Bird No. Because the conference would hate that.

Fortune They would absolutely hate it.

Bird But they don't mind saying: keep the nig-nogs out of the country . . . sorry, euphemisms, keep the euphemisms out of the country . . .

Fortune Keep the euphemisms out of the country, because then that becomes a British policy, and we can be proud of it.

Bird Racism should be British racism.

Fortune Absolutely.

Bird Where does the Prime Minister himself personally stand on this?

Fortune Well of course this isn't a personal responsibility of the Prime Minister, it's a departmental matter, but he has a duty of course, as Prime Minister, to delegate racism and xenophobia to his ministers . . .

Bird To his ministers?

Fortune Yes, because his first duty is to appear

to be a very nice man, and stay on as Prime Minister for as long as possible.

Bird George Parr, thank you very much for coming to talk to us.

RAIL

We did this in October 1994, just after the end of the prolonged rail strike, which cost British Rail £200 million. At that time Railtrack's assets were valued at something over £6 billion; when it was privatized in May 1996 the Government sold it off for £1.9 billion. It seems that Bob Horton had worked his old BP magic once again.

Fortune Bob Horton, you're the Chairman of Railtrack.

Bird Oh I can see you don't pull your punches. Yes, all right, all right, if you want to ask embarrassing questions, that's fine with me. Fine . . .

Fortune No, I . . .

Bird Absolutely, if you want to play rough I'll play rough . . .

Fortune . . . I'd really, I'd really like to talk about top management.

Bird Yes?

Fortune The way in which a breed of top managers like yourselves, whose skills have been honed in the private sector . . .

Bird Yes.

Fortune Are being recruited by the Government to look at rather moribund, public, old fashioned . . .

Bird . . . yes, corporations. Inefficient, slack, over-manned, feather-bedded public corporations.

Fortune Exactly.

Bird And that's what they've called me in to do, because I'm a rough, tough, hands on, hard-nosed er . . .

Fortune Abrasive.

Bird Abrasive, abrasive manager. I've got a harder nose than most people around.

Fortune And of course you used to be Chairman of BP.

Bird Yes, I was Chairman and Chief Executive of BP, and while I was there I really made a difference. If I come into an organisation they say, you know, Bob Horton takes it over,

Bob Horton shakes it up, makes the pips squeak.

Fortune Because you had a lot of experience didn't you, with BP in America?

Bird Yes, well that's where I learnt about what being a manager really is. You see the Americans' idea of a business man is a man who's imbued with a culture of success, who is efficient, who is competitive, and who is of course very highly rewarded, and now we wanted to bring that culture over to British industry.

Fortune And what did you start with?

Bird Well we started with the high rewards. We thought, we'll see what the high rewards do, and there might be some efficiency in one or two other things, but if we're lucky they will follow.

Fortune Absolutely, and you were paid as Chairman and Chief Executive of BP £800,000 a year . . .

Bird £800,000 a year when I was Chairman, yes.

Fortune But you did make a difference?

Bird I did make a tremendous difference.

When I left BP in June 1992 BP's profits for that year were £112 million.

Fortune And what were their profits when you joined the company?

Bird When I became Chief Executive and Chairman two years before that they were £2·8 billion.

Fortune So in effect, in just over two years, you lost the company two and a half billion pounds.

Bird Well I'm not very good at figures, but it's probably something of that order. But I did make a difference, you see, I mean I . . .

Fortune And then of course you were asked to resign?

Bird No, I'd like to set the record straight on that, my fellow Directors on the Board of BP, Sir Patrick Sheehy, and one or two others, called me in for a perfectly routine meeting on Sunday morning, and they they put to me a hypothetical question, they said: 'Look, Bob, if you were a Director of a company and there was a chap working in this company . . .'

Fortune Uh huh.

Bird '. . . who had made a *catastrophic* balls-up of the job . . .'

Fortune Of the whole job, yes . . .

Bird '. . . what would you do?' So I said: 'Well of course I'd fire him.'

Fortune You would fire him?

Bird Oh absolutely, yes. Well I fired thirty thousand people when I was at BP, so one more wouldn't make much difference.

Fortune No. So did you . . . ?

Bird So I said: 'Yes, bring him to me and I'll fire him.' And he said: 'No, it's you Bob.'

Fortune Oh I see, yes.

Bird And I said: 'Well I'm sorry, I don't want to go, I mean there are things I want to do still at BP.'

Fortune That's what they were afraid of?

Bird Exactly, yes. Yes. So they said: 'Well what would it take, how much money would it take to get you out of here?'

And I said: 'I'm not interested in money, I'm really not interested in money, but a million and a half would probably do it.'

Fortune A million and a half.

Bird Yes . . .

Fortune Which is what you got.

Bird That's what I got, yes, for redundancy . . .

Fortune Now that seems to me an awful lot of money . . .

Bird Oh no.

Fortune . . . frankly. I mean do you think you were worth that?

Bird Absolutely worth it, look, well I mean, if you had lost your company £2·6 billion in two years I think one and a half million pounds is very little to pay to stop you working there and doing any more damage . . .

Fortune I can see that makes sense. And then of course, not long after that you were head-hunted by the Government . . .

Bird By the Government, yes.

Fortune . . . to head up Railtrack.

Bird Yes, after the privatization of the railways, they wanted somebody to run the one public sector part of the railways that was left, you see, they wanted somebody to bring in this, you know . . .

Fortune . . . the discipline of the market and . . .

Bird . . . and and the private sector aura of success.

Fortune Yes . . . And have you made a difference in your new job?

Bird I've made a tremendous difference. I've only been there, well six months now, but we've already lost two hundred million pounds.

Fortune You have . . .

Bird And another two hundred million pounds of course has been lost to industry as a result of of . . .

Fortune This is all to do with the strike of course?

Bird Yes, but it won't be just that, it will probably be more than that.

Fortune Because British Rail will want compensating won't they, for the lack of business during the strike.

Bird That's right, so it could be anything up to five hundred million pounds. So I mean people had never heard of Railtrack when I took it over, but they have now.

Fortune That's true. Looking back at the strike, which is over now of course, would you have done anything different at all?

Bird Well no I don't think so. I went on holiday when it started, and . . .

Fortune Well you'd only been working there for about two months . . .

Bird Yes, I was very exhausted, it was a very stressful time, so I went on holiday to France, and then I came back, which some people thought was a mistake, but I did offer to speak to Mr Knapp . . .

Fortune Uh huh.

Bird At any time.

Fortune Yes.

Bird Absolutely any time, I said I would talk to Mr Knapp at any time. Well not on Thursdays, because I don't work on Thursdays.

Fortune No, or Fridays.

Bird No, I don't work on Fridays, I only work a three-day week at . . .

Fortune For which you are being paid £120,000 a year, is that right?

Bird Well exactly you see, so it shows that I don't do everything for money . . .

Fortune You do it for the challenge . . .

Bird . . . I just do it for the love of it, and for the challenge, yes.

Fortune Absolutely.

Bird Otherwise I wouldn't work for peanuts, let's put it like that, would I?

Fortune That's very true. It is true, however, isn't it, to say that at the beginning of the strike you did offer the signalmen 5.6 per cent as a means of settling the dispute?

Bird No no I . . . no we didn't.

Fortune Oh you didn't?

Bird No. No, we never offered that.

Fortune You can say categorically that you never did.

Bird Absolutely, yes.

Fortune Yes.

Bird Or, well, let me put that in a slightly different way. Yes we did offer it. We did offer it, but it was offered not by me, but by somebody at a slightly lower level of management.

Fortune Can I just make this point; has it ever occurred to you that perhaps there might be a different agenda here?

Bird In what way?

Fortune Well hasn't it ever occurred to you that perhaps the Government, who are notoriously anti-rail, head-hunted you because of your track record . . .

Bird Hmmm.

Fortune . . . and thought that if they left you in charge of it the railway system would eventually come to its knees, and they they could say: We can't go on pouring money into this, it's not working. And then they could sell off the assets, the land, the stations, and everything else for a knock-down price of a few billion pounds, and then announce some tax cuts with the proceeds?

Bird Yes, I suppose that's possible. Yes, I suppose, but I don't think they're as clever as that.

Fortune Bob Horton, thank you very much.

BUDGET

This was done in the week prior to Kenneth Clarke's 1995 Budget. It is a philosophical piece about democratic choice, or, as it is technically known, tax cuts.

Fortune George Parr, you're very closely involved in the preparation of the Budget.

Bird Yes, I've been working with the Chancellor and the Treasury team on its final stages.

Fortune Now I do realise that nothing at all could induce you to reveal secrets of the Budget.

Bird Oh no, no. Well, very large sums of money, but otherwise no, because actually the final calculations haven't been made yet.

Fortune I see. Of course you're an economist.

Bird No, no, I work for Euro Disney. I've been seconded to the Treasury for this period.

Fortune I can't quite see the connection between a fantasy theme park and the Budget.

Bird Can't you? I thought it was staring you in the face. Well, no, the connection is, people go to Euro Disney, and they see the enchanted palace and the crocodile pool and the wild west saloon, but they don't think they've really been there until they see the twelve-foot-high figure with the long white whiskers and the big black ears.

Fortune I see, yes.

Bird You see? And in the same way, this Budget is just before a general election. Now during the general election you will hear a lot of discussion about education and health and unemployment.

Fortune Hmmm.

Bird But people won't feel they really know how to vote until they know what sort of tax cut they're going to have.

Fortune So the tax cut is so to speak the mouse in your analogy.

Bird	It's the mouse, it's the cheese, it's the trap. It's the thing, you see, which is going to decide whether people vote for the Conservative Party or not.
Fortune	And you think that you're qualified to know what is going to make them vote in that way?
Bird	Well I've spent the last few years getting people to travel hundreds of miles to a swamp outside Paris, to see a pointless farrago of overpriced trivia, and so I think I do know what the public are inclined to fall for.
Fortune	And in this case of course it's the tax cut.
Bird	Yes.
Fortune	But I mean people are saying already, aren't they, that if the Chancellor cuts taxes it's a simple bribe?
Bird	Well, as we all know, the general public are inclined to jump to wild conclusions in a hurry, but in this case they're right.
Fortune	So it is, it is just bribery?
Bird	It is just bribery, yes.

Fortune But surely there must be, I mean a sort of fig leaf of economic argument which says that cutting taxes would actually improve the economy.

Bird Well there may be I suppose, I don't know. We haven't discussed that in the Treasury, we've just discussed the bribing side of things.

Fortune I see. But aren't the electorate going to despise the Government which just offers them bribes?

Bird Well this is the calculation that we have to make. At the moment you see this is a fine calculation. Do they despise us more than we despise them? I mean they know it's a bribe, and we know that they know it's a bribe, and they know that we know that they know it's a bribe, but it's a matter of pitching the bribe at just the right level. I mean just let me shape the figures: if it's one pence in the pound off income tax, people will say: 'well this is just a bribe and I'm not going to vote for anything as shameless as that.' But if it's three pence off the income tax, they say: 'well this is just a bribe, but it's a bloody good one.' And so they vote for it. You see what I'm getting at?

Fortune Yes, I do, I'm seeing the logic, yes.

Bird Good.

Fortune Except then in that case you might as well offer them anything, couldn't you, offer them the moon?

Bird Oh well no, in that case the calculation goes: instead of do we despise them for being greedy, it's do we despise them for being stupid, because they know that if we cut the top rate income tax from 40 per cent to 5 per cent say, which is what the very high earners pay anyway, then they'll know it's not going to work. I mean they know that we think they're stupid, but it's important that they don't think we think they're as stupid as all that.

Fortune And in any case, presumably, if the tax cuts don't help the economy, you're going to have to put up taxes again in a couple of years?

Bird Well . . .

Fortune Which is what happened last time.

Bird Well of course that's the risk you take. It's like the Lottery really, it *is* a lottery in fact; people know they're not going to have much chance of winning the Lottery, but they know that unless they buy the card they're not going to have any chance at all, in the same way they know the tax cuts probably won't work, but they're not going to get them unless they vote Conservative. You follow me, you are following me?

Fortune Yes, I'm . . . yes. We seem to have stumbled into a world of complete cynicism here, have we?

Bird Unfortunately, we all know that it is a very cynical world, and rightly or wrongly, everybody despises politicians. But that's a tremendous advantage to us. Because, you're not keeping up here, because the Chancellor knows that people *already* despise him because he's a politician, so they aren't going to *start* despising him, because he gives money away in bribes, are they? Let me draw you an analogy. The Chancellor, in this case, is a drug dealer. And the voter is an addict, you see. Now, the addict may despise the drug dealer.

Fortune Lowest form of human life.

Bird Yes. But he's still quite glad to see him coming round the corner with his little bag of white powder, isn't he? You see? . . . I'm not saying of course that the Chancellor *is* a drug dealer . . .

Fortune No no, no no . . .

Bird I have no way of knowing whether he is or not.

Fortune No. But is it, am I being just, I'm sorry, sort of hopelessly idealistic . . .

Bird Hmmm.

Fortune . . . to think that the electorate would actually prefer politicians who had some principles, and who stuck to the promises that they made?

Bird That would be disastrous.

Fortune Would it?

Bird Oh yes, that isn't what it takes. Look, Britain at the moment is in a relatively good economic position. We've got growth at 2 per cent and a relatively low rate of inflation. Now the reason that we are in that good position is because in 1992 we left the European Exchange Rate Mechanism and devalued the pound. Both of which things John Major, the Prime

Minister, said he would never do, he promised he would never do it and if he did do it, it would be a complete betrayal of the country.

Fortune So it's only because John Major did betray the country that we're as well off as we are now?

Bird Yes, you're getting there, yes.

Fortune So this means, I'm gradually learning this argument, this means that we should vote for the party which is most likely to break its promises on principle?

Bird [LAUGHS] If only it was as simple as that the world would be a much better place. No, you can't do that because you never know in advance which principles you have to break, you see, that's the thing.

Fortune It's not until you've abandoned a principle that you know whether it's going to . . .

Bird . . . whether it's going to work or not. Yes, exactly right.

Fortune And of course I suppose in some senses the electorate too can't be relied on to . . .

Bird Well no, we say that the voters despise the Government for not keeping its promises, but then the voters don't keep their promises either, do they?

Fortune No. Because in the last election people said they'd be prepared to pay more tax for better public services, and then when it came to it they actually voted for lower taxes.

Bird Yes. They said they would vote Labour, they told the opinion polls that they'd vote Labour, and then of course they went and voted Conservative, and you know, this is very, makes it very difficult for somebody . . .

Fortune It's very difficult to predict anything.

Bird . . . for somebody like me, yes. Because if you can't rely on these people in this way . . . and the thing that worries us is that Mr Blair is bringing the Labour Party to the point where I think it might well be possible, he may have already achieved this, that people will be ashamed to say they're going to vote for the Labour Party as well. Which will be a big step forward for them.

Fortune But that's democracy isn't it?

Bird That is democracy, yes. After all, it's a secret ballot.

Fortune It's a secret ballot, yes, and people have the right to vote for something they're deeply ashamed of.

Bird But it does make it difficult.

Fortune And of course you could have a situation where people took the bribe, took the tax cuts and still voted Labour, couldn't you?

Bird I suppose so . . .

Fortune How would you feel about that?

Bird Well I don't know, I'd give up then really. It would make me lose all my faith in human nature if that happened. I'd be inclined to go and live abroad if that was the case. Actually I do live abroad. And you never get this problem in the Cayman Islands, because you don't pay tax anyway.

Fortune George Parr, thank you very much indeed.

Bird That's all right, it's a pleasure.

CONDOMS

Unknown to us, Friday 10 November 1995 was Aids Awareness Day. We were in the studio preparing to record our piece for the Rory Bremner show when somebody rang from Channel 4 asking if we could do some little exchanges for showing between other programmes on the subject of the use of condoms. This isn't our normal territory, but we came up with the following snippets.

Q: Sir George Parr, can I ask you: when it comes to sex, what do you do about protection?
A: I've got a very good accountant, he makes sure the overheads are kept down.

Q: When it comes to sex, what sort of birth control do you use?
A: Just watch.
Q: Why, are you going to demonstrate?
A: No, I mean I just watch, that's the safest way I find (and my wife prefers it).

Q: When it comes to sex, what sort of birth control do you use?
A: I leave all that to my wife.
Q: You mean she chooses which method?

A: No, I leave the sex to my wife. She prefers it like that, at least that's what she tells me.

Q: Sir George Parr, do you employ condoms?
A: As long as they've got a proper work permit, I don't care where they come from.

DEREGULATION (Health & Safety)

At the 1993 Conservative Party Conference the then Minister at the DTI in charge of deregulation, Neil Hamilton, held up a printout of the list of orders and regulations which, being 'a burden on British industry', were about to be abolished by the Government. Our piece is a meditation on that subject. Neil Hamilton himself was abolished by the government a year later.

Fortune George Parr, you're a businessman . . .

Bird That's right.

Fortune So you'll be very pleased by the announcement in the Queen's Speech that a lot of petty regulations are going to be taken away from businessmen like yourself.

Bird Yes. I, I'm absolutely delighted about it, because my business has been crippled by all these, these ridiculous regulations and and laws and . . .

Fortune You're in the food business aren't, you?

Bird Yes, that's right.

Fortune You make Parr's Gourmet Pies for Particular Palates.

Bird That's right.

Fortune Is that right?

Bird We make meat pies, and . . .

Fortune Which is a very very very competitive business.

Bird A very competitive business, and our margins are very tight. And I really need a lot of help from the Government, not a lot of obstruction, people coming in and telling me what I can and what I can't do, and strangling me with red tape.

Fortune I see. Can you give me an example of the kind of petty regulation which you . . .

Bird Well yes, I get inspectors coming around to the factory all the time, and they say: 'I want to inspect your lavatories.'

Fortune Yes.

Bird And I say: 'Well you can't. We haven't got any lavatories.' And . . .

Fortune Why, why is that exactly?

Bird It wouldn't work, because they, my workforce, they've got all that at home, so they don't need them, and then the inspectors say: 'Well where are your washing facilities?'

Fortune Exactly.

Bird And I say: 'We haven't got any washing facilities.'

Fortune But people, presumably, in the food industry, need to wash their hands when they've been to the lavatory?

Bird Well, we don't have any lavatories.

Fortune Oh yes.

Bird So there's no point in that. So that's exactly the kind of nonsense that we have to deal with.

Fortune It seems a sort of basic nonsense.

Bird Yes, that's right. And then there's the question, on the one hand they say, the workers have got to have protective clothing.

Fortune Yes.

Bird And on the other hand they say, isn't the temperature here, inside the factory, higher than it should be according to the regulations, a hundred and three degrees.

Fortune Well that seems quite . . .

Bird And I say: 'well you can't have it both ways. I mean you can't expect people to work in a hundred and three degrees and wear overalls.'

Fortune Because they'd be even hotter.

Bird Yes, they would be, my people are very happy in their shorts and singlets. And of course, being all Bangladeshis, that's what they're used to, because, that sort of heat . . .

Fortune You say your workforce is mainly Bangladeshis, that's . . .

Bird It's all Bangladeshi..

Fortune That's presumably so that you have a homogeneous workforce, and . . .

Bird That's right.

Fortune And a sort of family atmosphere.

Bird Very much a family atmosphere, and,

and they would tell the inspectors, if they could speak English, that they don't need these things, and of course they have a very realistic attitude towards pay and conditions, the Bangladeshis.

Fortune Do they?

Bird And towards the immigration laws.

Fortune What sort of immigration . . . ?

Bird Well I give them a choice, I say: 'do you want to work for 35p an hour, or do you want to be on the first boat back to Bangladesh, the poorest country in the world?' And of course, they take the right decision.

Fortune And they go on working.

Bird Yes.

Fortune So they're not too worried about the conditions in your factory?

Bird Oh no no, they love it. You see there's a lot of things about the machinery, for example . . .

Fortune Yes, the Health and Safety at Work Act.

Bird The Health and Safety at Work Act, and that says you must have guards on, for example, the gristle-pounding machine. And now the gristle-pounding machine is a machine which is very central to our meat pies, and it's a big sort of vat, with a lot of blades, razor-sharp blades, whirling round at tremendous speed, pounding the gristle.

Fortune Pounding the gristle. Well presumably they insist on you having guards around this machine.

Bird Well, but how can they push the gristle into the machine you see, if they can't be close, and of course they, our workforce want to be close to the machine, they like to see it working, and they like to be able to see where their fingers are, when they lose them, because this occasionally of course does happen, and they're very attached to their fingers. Only emotionally of course.

Fortune In a sentimental sense.

Bird And they need to see which is theirs and which is the person next door's.

Fortune Yes. Can I just comment here that surely all these regulations, now they're taken away . . .

Bird Yes?

Fortune . . . will be replaced by the market itself.

Bird Well that's exactly right.

Fortune Won't that in itself regulate towards safety standards, because . . .

Bird Of course, yes.

Fortune For example, if I, I mean to take an extreme example, if I buy one of your gourmet pies and I slice it open and find a severed finger . . .

Bird A finger inside . . .

Fortune . . . inside it . . .

Bird You wouldn't buy . . .

Fortune I wouldn't buy another one of your pies.

Bird Well we have, we have rigorous procedures in place . . .

Fortune Yes.

Bird . . . Yes we do, which is a man at the

end of the line looking in the pies as they come by, and doing what we call 'spotting the finger', and picking it out, and he does a very very good job. And of course we believe that the consumer also doesn't need mollycoddling, and protecting. 'Let the buyer beware', that is my motto.

Fortune Yes.

Bird And, or as the Latin tag is 'Cave canem'.

Fortune But that actually means 'Beware of the dog', doesn't it?

Bird Well yes, that too, we do mean that, in, rather . . .

Fortune Why would that be? Are you implying that, that dogs have something to do with your meat pies?

Bird Well, there is the occasional . . . But we do take the fur off, and, and the collar of course, if there is one.

Fortune That would be a job that the man at the end of the production line could . . .

Bird Oh no, that's before it gets into the gristle-pounding machine. But the other thing is they say hard hats.

Fortune What?

Bird Must be wearing hard hats in a food factory . . .

Fortune That sounds absolutely ridiculous if you're just making pies.

Bird Yes. Well exactly, and they say it's just because the roof is coming in, is collapsing, and I say, it's made of asbestos, it's very light. And anyway, it just, well it drifts down, the powder . . .

Fortune Sort of, yes . . .

Bird The Bangladeshis love it, they've never seen snow, and they think it's . . .

Fortune It's a sort of Christmassy scene.

Bird Yes.

Fortune For them.

Bird Yes, for them, they absolutely love it.

Fortune Well these obviously are ways of cutting down your overheads aren't they?

Bird Yes.

Fortune And are you going to comply with export labelling regulations?

Bird Well that's another thing you see, I mean it doesn't end in the factory, all this stupid legislation and regulations, it goes on, I mean, they tell us to be competitive, they tell us to go out and market, and yet at the same time they want truth in labelling, which means I've got to put on my pies . . .

Fortune Uh huh.

Bird 'Gourmet meat pies, ingredients: gristle, old bits of fat, putrefied dog and occasional fingers.'

Fortune Not to mention the asbestos, which is . . .

Bird The asbestos, yes, I have to put that down, yes.

Fortune So now you won't have to do that any more?

Bird No no.

Fortune Well that sounds . . . That sounds like a step forward, in your terms.

Bird I think it is, I mean I think that we have to to ask, when did British industry rule the world? A hundred years ago.

Fortune Well I suppose, in the nineteenth century, yes.

Bird A hundred years ago we led the world, and at the same time we led the world in sweated labour, sweat shops, child labour, starvation wages, long hours . . .

Fortune Slavery.

Bird And slavery, yes. And now it is not a coincidence I think, that those two things are together. Back to basics, that's what I say . . .

Fortune So you're talking about going back to basics?

Bird Back to basics, yes.

Fortune Yes. But, wouldn't it be true to say that someone who takes your, your view of these, of these matters, would be condoning nowadays having children working down the coal mines?

Bird Well we might still have coal mines if

we had children working down them.

Fortune Thank you very much George Parr.

THE ELDERLY

In Norman Lamont's Budget of 1993 it was proposed that VAT would be imposed on domestic fuel in two stages: 8 per cent in 1994 and 17.5 per cent the following year. As it happened, the latter increase was voted down in Parliament; we did the following piece in 1994, just after the Budget which introduced the 8 per cent level.

Fortune George Parr, you're the Director of a well-known independent think-tank, and you've been struggling with the problems involved in an aging population.

Bird That's right.

Fortune Now in the Budget this week, of course, the most controversial aspect was the imposition of VAT on fuel oil.

Bird Yes.

Fortune This is going to hit the pensioners very hard.

Bird Very hard, very hard.

Fortune And yet the Chancellor has offset that increase, hasn't he, by, by putting up old age pensions by what is it, 70p a week?

Bird Ha ha ha.

Fortune So what do you think of that?

Bird Well it's pathetic isn't it, I mean it's absolutely pathetic and, well outrageous frankly. The Government just keeps throwing money at this problem, without any thought really of . . . well the cost, what these old people should cost. I mean why should we automatically go on heating up these old people? Does it make them more efficient, will they contribute more to society when they're hotter?

Fortune So, what you're suggesting is some kind of cost benefit analysis of elderly people?

Bird Yes, I think we need that, and we need to know, like any other resource, how much it costs, and what use is it? Are they *any* use, old people?

Fortune Well the traditional view, surely, has been that old people represent a reservoir of wisdom in society, somewhere where young people can go and gain benefit from their vast experience.

Bird Yes, yes, that would be all right in old societies where nothing changed very much over the years, over the generations, but the contemporary world changes so fast, and the young people need to know things which will help them to prosper and flourish in a contemporary society. What do old people know about Pulp and Blur, and glue sniffing, and stacking shelves at Safeway, and things like that? Old people know nothing about that you see, they're completely useless.

Fortune Hufty.

Bird Pardon? Yes, Hufty, yes.

Fortune Yes, they know nothing.

Bird They know nothing about Hufty, I don't know very much about it myself.

Fortune No no. I can't say that I do.[1] So, so

[1] Hufty, for those with shorter memories, was a bald lesbian presenter on *The Word*, a Channel 4 youth programme. By coincidence, it was made for some of the time in the same studio building and on the same night as the Rory Bremner shows and Hufty's dressing room was next to ours. We never had the opportunity of conversation with her.

what you're saying, in effect, is that these elderly people have nothing to contribute, is that true?

Bird Well I happen to know, because I am a Director of a chain of old people's homes in the North of England, and so I have experience of these things, and old people just talk nostalgically about the Blitz and you know, sharing each other's ration cards and not locking their doors at night, and how wonderful it was in the old days, and all that sort of thing.

Fortune Mucking in.

Bird Mucking in, yes. There's very . . . young people don't need to know that, young people know how to compete with their neighbours don't they, now, not how to go round lending them cups of sugar, and things of that kind.

Fortune Doing the dirty on them.

Bird Yes, I mean so as far as I can see, all old people do is sit around old people's homes dribbling and and constituting a fire hazard.

Fortune Although, in some senses, the fire

hazard would be helped by the dribbles, wouldn't it?

Bird In what . . .

Fortune It would be a sort of primitive form of a sprinkler system.

Bird Well yes. Yes, in our old people's homes, it would be the only form, primitive or otherwise.

Fortune And I suppose incontinence would come into play here?

Bird In extreme emergencies, yes. In fact I've often heard: 'Mrs Hopkins come down, there's a conflagration in the basement, and we'd be very grateful for your input, and even more so for your output.'

Fortune Yes.

Bird Yes, sorry, we've rather lost track here.

Fortune What I was going to ask you really is that, is that what your proposal is going to involve here? I mean, are we talking about taking measures of some kind?

Bird Well I think we have to take

measures, I mean we need to have young people who are adapted . . . who are adaptable, I'm sorry, to changing circumstances. I mean, the New Testament shows us that, Christ for example, Jesus Christ I'm talking about.

Fortune In what sense?

Bird He was very adaptable, you know, he was trained as a carpenter.

Fortune Ah.

Bird And when the bottom fell out of the carpentry trade he diversified into the service industry. He started with a few loaves and fishes and built himself up into a medium-sized catering company.

Fortune And of course he didn't actually go on to be old either, did he?

Bird No he didn't, he died at thirty-three.

Fortune And of course being God he could decide when he was going to die, presumably.

Bird Yes, he could.

Fortune So you think that there is a sort of

message in that, that old age is not necessarily a good thing?

Bird Christ is a role model I think, in many respects.

Fortune Yes.

Bird I've always admired his work, except that I've always wished he looked a little more like Peter Lilley and a little less like Gerry Adams. But let me put this another way.

Fortune Yes?

Bird How many drooling old crones have you seen in the VIP lounge at Heathrow airport? Not very many is the answer.

Fortune No, I don't, sorry, I can't quite see what this is . . .

Bird Well there you are, the people you see in the VIP lounge at Heathrow airport are the people who are valuable to society. They are the wealth creators, the top businessmen, and the irony of it is they have a lower life expectancy, because of the pressures on them.

Fortune Oh I see, they're making all these

corporate decisions all the time, so they don't . . .

Bird The average businessman, by the time he gets to Heathrow airport, has already had a harrowing time, worrying about whether his chauffeur's going to get there in time or whether he's going to have to kick his heels in the bar for two and a half hours waiting for the next plane. And when he gets on the plane, is there going to be enough leg room in his first class seat, is the stewardess going to be attractive enough, is the champagne going to be cold enough, when he gets to the other side is his hotel swimming pool going to be of an adequate size, is his suite going to have a decent view? Is the executive trouser press going to be functioning? You see all these, these myriad considerations which weigh upon the top businessman.

Fortune Whereas what you're saying is that the elderly don't have these intense pressures on them.

Bird No, exactly. The working-class elderly are fed and watered by the welfare state, so nothing wears out. They don't have any sense of stress, so in a way you see the wrong genes survive.

Fortune I'm sorry isn't that, isn't that rather getting a bit close to eugenics?

Bird No no no, I don't think so. That's an abhorrent idea.

Fortune Yes.

Bird Eugenics. But although the State shouldn't intervene in that way, the State shouldn't intervene in the opposite way either, prolonging these rather pointless lives by heaping these hand-outs on them.

Fortune 70p a week.

Bird 70p a week, exactly.

Fortune Yes, I can see that. So, is there something that can be done in your view?

Bird Well it's not an easy problem, and I don't pretend to have the answer. I mean I do think there *is* an answer, somewhere floating around, but I've never been able to quite put my finger on it. It's a difficult . . . it's a very difficult problem.

Fortune Well I'm almost relieved that there isn't a solution, because it almost sounded as if you were talking about culling the elderly.

Bird That's it! That's the answer! That's the idea I think I have been looking for all this time, yes, yes.

Fortune Surely one can't, one can't imagine sort of bands of DHSS death squads roaming around shooting . . .

Bird No no. No they couldn't, they'd bungle it, they're civil servants. No, this should be left to market forces, along with everything else.

Fortune In what sense?

Bird People should have the choice, a choice should be offered to people.

Fortune Hmmm. So . . .

Bird Not the old people of course, I'm talking about their families, their families should be given a choice.

Fortune I see, so let me summarize, what you're saying is that the State should no longer be responsible at all for elderly people.

Bird Yes.

Fortune They should be the sole responsibility of their families?

Bird Yes, the families have to balance their priorities, they must ask themselves fundamental questions: do we want the new Mondeo, or do we want granny hanging around leaving her colostomy bag on the hostess trolley?

Fortune Yes, well, that is a very personal view Sir George . . .

Bird It is, yes.

Fortune . . . and I wonder . . .

Bird I remember my own mother saying to me: 'George, I do not want to become a burden on the Public Sector Borrowing Requirement.'

Fortune Very public-spirited of her. But might I ask you, since you're not yourself Sir George in the first flush of youth, what is actually going to happen to you in ten or fifteen years?

Bird Well I can promise you this, I myself, I am not going to be a burden on future generations.

Fortune So you're, you're talking about euthanasia?

Bird No, I'm talking about Greece. I have a property in Greece, and I shall go and spend my retirement there. Greece is a country which respects the old, which is of course why it's so pathetically backward economically.

Fortune Sir George Parr, thank you very much.

EUROFIGHTER

Very expensive weapons systems are an ideal subject for comedy and over the year the British Ministry of Defence has been at the forefront in designing, specifying or purchasing equipment with an eye to its comic potential. Back in the sixties when we worked at Peter Cook's *Establishment* club we used to do a sketch which involved giving a perfectly straightforward account of British defence policy: it invariably brought the house down.

All the facts presented in the following piece are true, but as it was performed in 1994 it is necessary to add a few millions, or even billions, to any cost figures quoted.

Fortune George Parr, you're a senior figure at the Ministry of Defence . . .

Bird Yes.

Fortune And after a week in which there's been a tremendous amount of emphasis on the rather sleazy side of the arms industry, it's very refreshing to meet someone with a story to tell which combines tremendous success and complete probity.

Bird	Yes, this is not a story of shady dealings, or wasting of taxpayers' money, this is something of which we can be proud of in Britain, this is the development of our new fighter aircraft . . .
Fortune	Ah . . .
Bird	. . . which is designed to protect our country, into the 21st century; it's done by the Government for the people.
Fortune	Yes, this is the European Fighter Aircraft.
Bird	The Eurofighter, yes.
Fortune	That's wonderful.
Bird	It is isn't it, and also it's a great example of something which is often derided which is, which is er er er um um . . . [1]
Fortune	The European allies have got together to build . . .
Bird	That's right.
Fortune	To build this aircraft.

[1] The long Section of blathering at this point is due to John Bird's inability to think of the word 'co-operation'.

Bird Yes, yes, sorry.

Fortune And that's a tremendous achievement in itself.

Bird Yes, yes.

Fortune Isn't it?

Bird It is a tremendous achievement.

Fortune Yes.

Bird And I think, you know, that we're at the cutting edge of . . . the Germans, the British, and ourselves have got together, no no sorry . . . The Germans, the British . . . we're the British aren't we?

Fortune We're the British, yes.

Bird It's the British, the Spanish, the Italians and the Germans. And we've all got together and for fifteen years we have been developing this, this wonderful new aircraft which is going to cost £32 billion and will be, when it's finished, if it ever is finished, the world's most advanced military aircraft.

Fortune And can you tell me something about the way that this co-operation works,

I mean who actually does what?

Bird Well, yes, we all, each country makes a different part of it. The Germans build the body and the tail, the British build the trunk, and the Italians build the legs and the tusks and the Spanish paint it white.

[PAUSE]

Bird I'm sorry, I don't know why I said that, I'm terribly sorry . . .

Fortune That can't be right, can it?

Bird . . . do you mind if I have Jumbo on my knee, because he makes me think straight, you know.

[PICKS UP TOY ELEPHANT AND HOLDS IT]

Fortune Yes.

Bird Don't you Jumbo? He said yes, you probably didn't hear him did you?

Fortune No I didn't. He was speaking elephant language?

Bird He speaks elephant language. Only we in the Ministry of Defence understand.

Fortune Yes.

Bird No actually the real story is, yes . . . I'll put you down Jumbo if that's all right [PUTS DOWN ELEPHANT] the real story is that the United Kingdom builds the front fuselage and half the right wing. The Germans build the centre fuselage and the tail fin, the Italians build the left wing and half the rear fuselage, and the Spanish build the other half of the right wing and the other half of the rear fuselage.

Fortune You're making this up.

Bird No, no, I'm not making it up. This actually is the truth, isn't that right Jumbo?

Fortune He says it is . . .

Bird In elephant language, yes.

Fortune Can you tell me perhaps what this aircraft was designed to do?

Bird Well I'm glad you asked that, because it's designed for a very specific task, it's designed to combat a very real threat from the Soviet Union, from two fighters the Soviet Union have, the MIG 29 and the Sukoi 27, which would be launched from East Germany.

Fortune Might it be objected that East Germany doesn't exist any more?

Bird That's a rather nit-picking attitude if I may say so. I think we should look at the big picture here, I mean this is a very, or going to be when it goes into service, well when it starts being built in 1996, it's going to be a wonderful aircraft, it's going to be a match I think for anything the Soviet Union can throw at us.

Fortune I don't want to nit-pick again, but . . .

Bird No no no.

Fortune The Soviet Union doesn't exist either does it?

Bird Well no, but neither does the Eurofighter yet, so we're very well matched.

Fortune Yes, might it be objected that in recent wars that we've fought in, like the Gulf and Bosnia, what we needed was ground attack aircraft . . .

Bird Yes, yes.

Fortune I mean after all, at the beginning of the Gulf War, Saddam Hussein withdrew his fighters didn't he?

Bird He did, he did, that's true, but if people don't fight wars properly, that's not our fault. It can be adapted this plane . . .

Fortune Oh it can be adapted?

Bird The Eurofighter can be adapted for . . .

Fortune For a ground attack role.

Bird For ground attack, yes, by putting heavier bombs on and heavier rockets . . .

Fortune I understand.

Bird Although there are one or two drawbacks to that.

Fortune Such as?

Bird It won't fly.

Fortune You mean that it will become completely unstable and crash?

Bird No no no, no it won't *crash*, because it won't take off. So we could . . .

Fortune You could use it on the ground, you could drive it along the ground . . .

Bird We could use it on the ground, we could drive it about . . .

Fortune Rather like a, like a tank . . .

Bird And fire at things, but it wouldn't be used to its best capability in that role I don't think . . .

Fortune No.

Bird Because like most aircraft it is at its best when it's flying about in the air.

Fortune Yes. Might it further be objected that now there isn't a threat from the Soviets that this aircraft is already rather out of date?

Bird Well no, it can't be out of date, it hasn't been built yet. It will only be out of date once it's built.

Fortune Yes.

Bird Don't forget that this programme was started in 1979 when there was a very real threat from the Soviet Union from the MIG 29s and so forth, and so it was very urgent that we we find an answer to that . . .

Fortune Desperate . . .

Bird And we did find it.

Fortune Yes.

Bird I mean you can't just snap your fingers and get a very sophisticated weapon here . . .

Fortune No of course not.

Bird It takes time and particularly when there are four countries coming together, I mean there were unforeseen problems . . .

Fortune Technical problems?

Bird Technical problems, exactly. For instance, it turned out we don't all speak the same language . . .

Fortune No. That's very true.

Bird Yes, and things like when we put the two halves of the right wing together we found that we'd used inches and the Spanish had used centimetres and so our, our half was twice as big as their half.

Fortune Yes, of course it would be. There are other tensions within the allies too, I believe the Germans are thinking, even at this moment, of pulling out altogether?

Bird Yes, they are thinking of doing that, but we could still go ahead. I mean we could try and and bolt the rear fuselage straight onto the front fuselage without having the middle bit, or the tail fin, I mean it would be cheaper if you did that.

Fortune It would be much cheaper, yes.

Bird I mean we wouldn't . . .

Fortune . . . and shorter.

Bird You'd need smaller hangars . . .

Fortune That's very true. But even if, even if by some miracle this aircraft actually did get off the ground, the point remains that it doesn't have an enemy to fight, does it?

Bird Well, no, but it costs £45 million, you know, this plane, so we don't want people shooting at it.

Fortune And the planes that would be shooting at it in any case are Russians . . .

Bird Yes.

Fortune And the Russian airforce is now our ally isn't it?

Bird That's perfectly true yes, but we have discovered, intelligence has told us, unfortunately, I'm sorry to have to say this, but the Russians have, in a rather sneaky and underhand manner been selling this plane, to, well anybody who would buy it really, so it could fall into the hands of crack-pot dictators, terrorist states, and we'd have a threat from them, which the Eurofighter can counter.

Fortune Have they actually sold it to anyone at the moment?

Bird Oh yes.

Fortune Oh they have?

Bird I mean just to name one, because there is only one, Malaysia.

Fortune But Malaysia is an ally of ours isn't it?

Bird Yes, yes, that's true, but we know that for one thing Malaysia is a heavily armed country, we know that because we've sold them the arms, and they're a very volatile little people . . .

Fortune Yes.

Bird And anything upsets them, I mean they got very upset just reading *The Sunday Times* last year. So . . .

Fortune So you can foresee a time when there would be aerial combat between the Eurofighter and say the MIG 29, over Malaysia?

Bird Not over Malaysia, no, because the Eurofighter can't fly that far. It doesn't have that big a range, but we'll have to persuade the Malaysians to come over to Europe and engage us over Europe. But they probably would, I mean as you say, they are allies, so . . .

Fortune Yes, they are allies . . .

Bird Yes, so they probably would do that, and of course there'd be advantages to them, they wouldn't get bits of aircraft falling onto their own population.

Fortune But if in either case there isn't a miraculous restoration of the Soviet Empire, or if Malaysia decides after all not to invade Europe can you see a role for this aircraft? What are we going to do with it?

Bird Well . . . we could sell it.

Fortune Well I thought you said that selling things like this was sneaky and underhand and uncivilised?

Bird No, that's, that's if the Russians sell it. If we sell it, it's exports.

Fortune Of course it is. And who would we sell it to?

Bird I don't mind, anybody, anybody. I mean, you know, sort of anybody who'd like it really, any kind of mad African dictator. I mean, you know, they wouldn't *have* to be African to buy it. They would have to be mad, though.

Fortune Sir George Parr, thank you very much indeed.

THE MILLENNIUM

Background data: The new millennium begins on 1 January 2000. For additional information on celebration plans, balloons, poison gas and other connected topics please ring the Millennium Commission on: 0171 340 2001

Bird In four years time we shall be celebrating the end of the twentieth century, and by a happy coincidence, the beginning of the twenty-first century, and George Parr, you have just been appointed the coordinator of the millennium celebrations, a sort of millennium supremo.

Fortune Yes.

Bird Of course there is a Millennium Commission . . .

Fortune Yes, but they're only responsible for events which will be funded by the National Lottery . . .

Bird Yes.

Fortune Whereas ideas have been coming

forward from private companies, and we're very pleased with this, but we feel there is a danger of a proliferation of unconnected events, and a need for an overall unifying vision.

Bird Vision, yes. What sort of ideas have been coming from private sources though?

Fortune Well, for example, Virgin Atlantic, as you may know, and British Airways have come up with truly imaginative schemes, which in themselves embody Britain's place at the leading edge of innovation in aircraft history.

Bird That's right, yes, British Airways are going to build a funfair wheel, aren't they?

Fortune Yes.

Bird Opposite the Houses of Parliament.

Fortune Yes, a very big wheel.

Bird Yes, a big wheel, this, this . . . how is this innovative say compared to an aeroplane?

Fortune Well, it'll go up.

Bird Yes.

Fortune And it'll come down again.

Bird Down again, yes.

Fortune And it'll go . . .

Bird Round and round.

Fortune Go round and round. And of course aircraft can do this.

Bird Yes, they can, yes.

Fortune But the innovative thing about this is that the wheel will do it very much slower.

Bird Yes . . .

Fortune And of course Richard Branson has another path-finding idea.

Bird Yes?

Fortune He's going to have a very large balloon.

Bird Is that going to go anywhere?

Fortune No, it's going to be tethered to the ground.

Bird This, this is . . .

Fortune But it's very very exciting.

Bird Very exciting isn't it, very exciting.

Fortune And it doesn't stop there.

Bird I was going to say, there hasn't been anything like this really since um, at all. Except possibly for the German Zeppelins of the First World War, and of course the big funfair wheel in Vienna, which was built in 1897.

Fortune Really?

Bird Yes.

Fortune Well, as I say, it doesn't stop there. Because, a consortium in the City is planning to build a tower, 650 feet high, costing £91 million called the Globorama.

Bird Globorama, yes, that name is redolent of class and dignity, isn't it?

Fortune It is.

Bird What will this building do? Is this building going to be tethered to the ground?

Fortune Well, hopefully.

Bird Yes, yes.

Fortune If there are any building inspectors left. But this building, people will be able to go into it and go up to the top of it and then high above London they will be shown live satellite television pictures of Sydney Harbour.

Bird That's terrific isn't it?

Fortune Very very exciting.

Bird Yes. Of course it will be dark in Sydney when they see it, but still it will be good, won't it?

Fortune It will be good.

Bird It'll make you feel proud to be British. Virginia Bottomley said that she wanted something, I can't remember exactly the phrase, to, to 'embrace the nation with a single vision', wasn't it?

Fortune Exactly, those were her very words.

Bird And are you doing anything in that respect?

Fortune Yes, it's a question really of finding an element in British Society which has the power to unite us and inspire us with affection and approval.

Bird That's almost impossible isn't it?

Fortune Well, it would seem to be, but we . . . we've actually come up with the Queen Mother.

Bird Yes, the Queen Mother, because, well, everybody loves the Queen Mother, don't they?

Fortune Yes, I think she's the last thing we have left that can unify us.

Bird Unify the nation, yes. The problem is, of course . . . I mean the Queen Mother is 96 years old, and without wishing to be pessimistic in any way, I mean I don't know quite how to put this, but I mean it's um, it is four years to go, isn't it, before, before . . . do you see, I mean I don't know whether you follow what . . .

Fortune Oh I see, yes, I see . . .

Bird So if she does peg out before that time, do you have a fall-back position on the Queen Mother at all?

Fortune Of course we do, yes. We have two approaches to this. The first is a giant hologram . . .

Bird Of her . . .

Fortune Of Her Majesty, which would be projected onto the night sky above London.

Bird This is tremendous, the sort of cutting edge of technology isn't it?

Fortune It will be, yes. We are already feeding the Queen Mother's coordinates into a computer programme . . .

Bird Yes.

Fortune . . . that will produce the the image.

Bird They must be very complex, the coordinates.

Fortune . . . very very complex. Yes.

Bird The hat alone is very . . .

Fortune Yes, I'm glad you mentioned the hat, because that's all we've managed to map, so far. And I'm afraid the hat alone is beginning to soak up our budget.

Bird So you won't be able to . . .

Fortune No, I don't think so, I think it's going to go through our cost ceiling.

Bird And will . . .

Fortune Well the second approach, the second approach is rather more low-tech. It involves a 300-foot-long inflatable replica of the Queen Mother, which will be towed across the London sky . . .

Bird Yes?

Fortune . . . hopefully by a Spitfire.

Bird Yes, I see.

Fortune Representing the the high-water point of British aircraft design.

Bird Yes, well I can see this in my mind's eye. The only thing is that the Spitfire is rather looking back, isn't it, on history as far as . . .

Fortune Well yes, and in fact the RAF is very keen to have a Tornado fighter bomber do this.

Bird You mean tow the inflatable Queen Mother . . .

Fortune Yes. But the idea of this structure passing over London at something like two thousand miles an hour . . .

Bird Yes.

Fortune . . . does present certain design difficulties.

Bird Some stresses on the Queen Mother.

Fortune There is, there is that possibility.

Bird I see.

Fortune And the possibility also of the whole replica breaking loose from the towing vehicle.

Bird That, well that would be a disaster wouldn't it, because . . .

Fortune Yes.

Bird . . . that might violate foreign air space, and . . .

Fortune Well there is that possibility of course, yes.

Bird And of course might cause a great problem, and also it might even become involved in an accidental way with the Richard Branson's balloon, for example, or . . .

Fortune Or even the ferris wheel.

Bird Or the ferris wheel.

Fortune Or even more disastrously, the Globorama tower.

Bird Yes, I can imagine that the last thing you need, as you're standing there looking at live pictures of Sydney harbour . . .

Fortune Yes, is some kind of collision with . . .

Bird . . . with a replica of the Queen Mother crashing through into the viewing platform. But, if we can just get off the Queen Mother for a moment, the the Millennium Commission do want to have a major exhibition, don't they, on a site in Greenwich?

Fortune That's right, they have chosen a site at Greenwich. Because the idea is that this project should demonstrate in some way some essential characteristic of the quality of life in this country at the moment.

Bird Of British life, yes. And what is this site in Greenwich in fact?

Fortune It's a site by the river, on the Greenwich peninsular, it's owned by British Gas, and it's at present derelict.

Bird Is it? By the river, it sounds perfect.

Fortune Oh it's wonderful. Absolutely wonderful. There is a slight drawback, in that it is very heavily polluted with cyanide and sulphur dioxide and other very toxic things . . .

Bird Because it was a gasworks?

Fortune It was a gasworks, yes.

Bird So this will represent Britain, as it were, will it?

Fortune Oh no. No, the whole site will have to be decontaminated.

Bird Oh, I see, and British Gas are going to clean it up are they?

Fortune No. No, there's a Government agency called English Partnerships which is going to put £20 million towards the clean-up of this land.

Bird When you say Government agency, it's taxpayers' money which is going to . . .

Fortune It's taxpayers' money, yes. And already English Partnerships are working very closely with British Gas, they have to.

Bird Yes.

Fortune And by a great stroke of luck, the Chairman of English Partnerships, Lord Walker, is also a director of British Gas.

Bird That's very lucky.

Fortune It is, terribly fortunate.

Bird There isn't any suggestion of conflict of interest, is there, here in this . . . ?

Fortune No, I wouldn't have thought so, no. Lord Walker has pointed out that during discussions about British Gas at English Partnerships he takes no part at all.

Bird What, he reads a book or something does he, and . . . ?

Fortune He looks out of the window . . .

Bird Looks out of the window, yes. Right, so they are going to clean up just the exhibition site, are they?

Fortune No, no, they'll clean up the whole of British Gas's land on the peninsular, I mean while the workers are there they may as well do that.

Bird Absolutely. And, will this have any, I mean the cleaning up of it, it will presumably effect the value of the land?

Fortune Well presumably, yes.

Bird What is the value now?

Fortune Nothing.

Bird Nothing. Because of the pollution of the gas . . .

Fortune Because of the pollution, yes.

Bird And when it's cleaned up?

Fortune When it's cleaned up, and the Jubilee Line extension has reached there . . . It should be worth between £250,000 and £500,000 an acre.

Bird Right, good, and what, what will happen after the exhibition is over, because it will only run for a year, won't it?

Fortune Yes, well after that . . .

Bird . . . I mean what happens to the land . . .

Fortune In fact British Gas has applied for, and been granted planning permission, and they're going to build three thousand houses and a business park and some shops.

Bird Well, that sounds a very good deal, considering the taxpayer is paying for for the cleaning up of the land, so . . .

Fortune Yes, but you must remember that British Gas itself is putting £20 million of their own money into the Jubilee Line extension.

Bird Oh I see, oh well that is, that's a lot of money.

Fortune It is.

Bird How much is the Jubilee Line extension going to cost all together?

Fortune £1·9 billion.

Bird Right, so that's quite a large proportion of that, um . . . Yes.

Fortune But it will increase the value of the land of course.

Bird To have the station there. Now I

understand that, that Sir Peter Levine is having trouble finding a company to raise the £400 million for the exhibition.

Fortune That is true.

Bird What will happen if he fails?

Fortune Well they won't get any Lottery money, and there won't be an exhibition.

Bird We shall be very disappointed of course.

Fortune And it will be very disappointing for British Gas. Because they won't get the revenue from the leases on the exhibition site, you see.

Bird No, but of course they'll still have the land, which . . .

Fortune They'll still have the land . . .

Bird Which has been cleaned up at taxpayers' expense . . .

Fortune Yes, and the planning permission.

Bird And the Jubilee Line built.

Fortune Yes, so they'll just have to bite the

	bullet and look on the bright side, won't they?
Bird	Indeed.
Fortune	They won't make £100 million, but they'll make £75 million, so . . .
Bird	But nevertheless, that whole thing will be very characteristic of Britain today, won't it really?
Fortune	In what way?
Bird	Well, that rather sums up Britain, that sort of thing.
Fortune	The exhibition?
Bird	No, this property deal.
Fortune	Oh I see, yes it does doesn't it? The land deal, yes.
Bird	Hmmm.
Fortune	I mean it's, it's evidence of of, what's the word, um . . . ?
Bird	. . . Enterprise?
Fortune	That's the word, yes.
Bird	And of course, if there is no

exhibition it will be very disappointing for the ordinary man and woman in the street too . . .

Fortune Yes, but we have a solution for that, if the exhibition doesn't take place, we're going to involve everyone in this country in a simple ceremony to mark the millennium.

Bird Which will consist of what?

Fortune Well, at midnight on the last day of the century Big Ben will chime and people will hear this on their radios and their television, and then afterwards Vera Lynn will sing 'There'll Always Be An England' and 'We'll Meet Again'. And then, at a given signal, everyone will get into bed, and pull the blankets over their heads, and stay there through the next day.

Bird Right, and that will be a very appropriate way for Britain to enter the twenty-first century. Thank you very much George Parr.

Fortune Thank you.

Apology

Nobody asked us to make this apology but we thought we'd do it anyway. Since we recorded this piece it has emerged that the cost of decontamination of the Greenwich site will be born not by English Partnerships and the taxpayer but by British Gas. In fact they are bound by law to pay for it since they were the original polluters; which makes it curious that British Gas didn't comment either on our piece or the newspaper article on which it was based.

However, further complications have now arisen in this saga. A sum of £85 million has floated into view which is the estimated cost of the provision of roads, sewers, landscaping and other infrastructure work. British Gas are apparently refusing to foot this bill on the grounds that they are already contributing enough. The Millennium Commission has said: 'We are aware of British Gas's position, but plans are proceeding on the assumption that the £85 million will be paid, whether by British Gas, English Partnerships, the Dept of the Environment or the commercial sector.'

Since we know that the commercial sector has so far been reluctant to invest in the exhibition itself they are unlikely to agree to pay for roads and sewers which will benefit only the owners of the site, and since the owners of the site are British Gas who are refusing to pay any more, that leaves English Partnerships and the Dept of the Environment. In other words, the taxpayer. The likelihood is, therefore, that the taxpayer will be paying not £20 million, as we suggested in our piece, but £85 million.

We would further like to apologise for suggesting that after the exhibition is dismantled the site will be worth £100 million to British Gas. At the time of going to press (July 1996), estimates of that figure put it at £200 million. (See *Financial Times*, July 8th 1996.) We very much regret our gross underestimation of British Gas's business acumen.